BURNING FIRES

Finding Treasures in Ashes

CRICKET SHILOH ANDERSON

Trilogy Christian Publishers
A Wholly Owned Subsidiary of Trinity Broadcasting Network
2442 Michelle Drive
Tustin, CA 92780

Copyright © 2020 by Cricket Shiloh Anderson

All Scripture quotations, unless otherwise noted, taken from THE HOLY BIBLE, NEW INTERNATIONAL VERSION®, NIV® Copyright © 1973, 1978, 1984, 2011 by Biblica, Inc.® Used by permission. All rights reserved worldwide.

Scripture quotations marked (KJV) taken from *The Holy Bible, King James Version*. Cambridge Edition: 1769.

All rights reserved, including the right to reproduce this book or portions thereof in any form whatsoever.

For information, address Trilogy Christian Publishing
Rights Department, 2442 Michelle Drive, Tustin, Ca 92780.
Trilogy Christian Publishing/ TBN and colophon are trademarks of Trinity Broadcasting Network.

For information about special discounts for bulk purchases, please contact Trilogy Christian Publishing.

Manufactured in the United States of America

Trilogy Disclaimer: The views and content expressed in this book are those of the author and may not necessarily reflect the views and doctrine of Trilogy Christian Publishing or the Trinity Broadcasting Network.

10 9 8 7 6 5 4 3 2 1

Library of Congress Cataloging-in-Publication Data is available.

ISBN 978-1-64088-927-9 (Print Book)
ISBN 978-1-64088-928-6 (ebook)

DEDICATION

To my daughter Trina Duran, my firstborn child, strong-willed and a fighter as evidenced through your instincts as a preemie to survive, God healed you. Love you, baby. You've traveled with me the longest. To my grandson, Andrew Duran, and son-in-law, Andy, love you very much.

To Donovan, my son, healed of deafness at age six during a Sunday night Communion Service. Thank you to the family of Pastor Charles Mc Hatton from Gospel Echoes who introduced me to the healing power of God. Thank you, anointed prayer and worship leader N. Randal Miller, Gospel Echoes. You taught me how to pray and worship our God and King. Donovan, you have a strong call on your life from God. Many pastors and leaders recognized and spoke of the call God on you when you were a youth. You will walk in and fulfill your God call. Don't forget to call your mom!

To all the Sunday School teachers who touch young lives. You may not know the impact you have made on a young life. To a Sunday school teacher at Ada First Baptist Church in Ada, Oklahoma. I don't know your name, but you gave me a very special gift. I remember you fondly. I was only six; (1961) you gave me a little white Bible for Easter. I don't have the Bible and couldn't read yet, but I do remember and thank you for your kindness. The gift gave me hunger and love for God's word. The little white Bible was my treasure.

To all the grandparents who touch young lives and my grandmother, Marietta Burgess who took me to church in Wetumka, Oklahoma. Because of you, I received Jesus Christ at age five. This encounter would help me live through the foster care programs and other life chaos. Thank you for the Wriggly chewing gum. You have been gone fifty years at this writing. I still buy Wriggly gum and remember you. I miss you.

CONTENTS

Acknowledgments 7
Introduction...9

Chapter 1: How Big Is Your God?..................................15
Chapter 2: When the World Peels You Like a Banana 22
Chapter 3: Is Your Tortoise Shell Too Small? 40
Chapter 4: Faith Is Like Planting a Carrot, You
Can't Keep Pulling It Up by the
Roots to See How It's Growing.....................60
Chapter 5: I Have the Chewing Gum, Do You
Have the Duct Tape? Let's Do This! 74
Chapter 6: Broken Records: Letting Go of the
Memories 82
Chapter 7: Who Told You that You Are Stupid?...........100
Chapter 8: In the Deep River? Turn Around
and Float Downstream for a While!............114
Chapter 9: Come to the Beach......................................127
Chapter 10: Bless This Mess!...135
Chapter 11: It Takes a Mountain to Climb 145
Chapter 12: Keep Your Lamp Plugged In.......................166
Chapter 13: This Card Is for Me.....................................174
Chapter 14: Blessed to Succeed, Succeed to Bless...........194

The Writer's Story 205
References 211

ACKNOWLEDGMENTS

Thank you to the powerhouse church 'Lite and Fire' in Surprise, Arizona. Thank you for the opportunity to pray and worship with all of you each week on Thursday and Sunday nights.

Thank you to Lite and Fire leadership, Pastors Jack and Deborah, the support team Ce Ci and Harry. You hold lightly, being good stewards of the presence of God. Because of your leadership in worship, we are a group of believers who are able to enter the throne room of God. Prayers are moving mountains when we seek His face together. Without your support, I would not have finished this writing assignment.

Thank you to Grace Bible Church in Sun City, Arizona; David Brainard; Pastors Bill Bjork, Charlie Dyer; usher team Joe French, Thomas Zubricky, Bud; and staff and volunteers David and Shirley Kettleson, Ken and Cherie Parsons, Pat Runyon, Alice and Sears.

Thank you for friends who were an encouragement, speaking with them rarely, yet knowing they were as close as a call: Corine Peck, Joyce Schlamp, and Nancy Braun.

Thank you to the following people who provided support and input for the completion of this writing: Arizona State, Danial Staab; Tempe, Lillia Sanchez-Gonzales; Avondale, Jessica Webb. Thank you to students and staff from

Midwestern Dental School and Gateway Beauty College, Paradise Valley. You listened to many hours of ideas for this workbook and helped me get ready for meetings.

I am grateful for Peoria Public Library system where I was able to spend hundreds of hours writing. The library provided a quiet room. Thankful for the space and time.

Thank you to God our Father, Jesus our Savior, and the Holy Spirit. Thank you for bringing me through the chaos and whirlwinds. In all this, I have learned to trust you. Because of you, my life is not a victim story but a proof of your abundant and tender love. Only you could take a child from living in group homes of foster care (an orphanage), save her also from domestic violence, and make her a child of the King. I thank you that you are the God, Savior, and healer who makes our mess into something you can use. Thank you that you take time to reveal to each of us our purpose.

Thank you to the editors and team at Trilogy Publishing. Thank you, Mark!

INTRODUCTION

If you have ever doubted God's love for you, experienced loss, have been abused, feel like a victim, are living in chaos or with chronic poverty, this book has been written for you. It is a workbook written and designed to bring healing to those who have been emotionally hurt, broken, and bruised by life and experiences. My desire is that it will bring hope to the lost or hurting and always point to God as a supreme partner in reaching your purpose-filled better life. Your past or where you started does not prove who you were created to be and does not dictate or stop your God-promised future.

I was asked to remove all scripture from this workbook with a promise that I would be allowed to bring the workbooks and workshops into state prisons and public programs. The offers were given with valuable reasoning and good intention. After prayer and much consideration, there was only one choice. If I removed the scripture, this would be just another program. I would be neglecting my assignment—the assignment God gave. Let God bring healing to those most hurt. I can just help to open the door to what God will do in a person's life. They are all children of the King almighty with all the rights of a king's inheritance.

History: After speaking with nonprofit directors of domestic violence and homeless shelters, they report that low self-esteem plagues shelter participants. Participants often return to an unhealthy environment out of fear, believing that they cannot live productively away from the abusive environment or without the addiction, and that they deserved or caused the abuse they have received. Discouragement and hopelessness foster a system where creativity and a better life seems unreachable. Living in a world of chronic poverty, neighborhood and school violence, experiencing child abuse, or living with chaos and trauma of divorce, death, or any loss can also contribute to a feeling of hopelessness. Many times, there are no positive role models to lead someone out of poverty and negative life cycles. Behaviors both negative and positive are learned in our life. Are you that pioneer that will help break the cycle of pain and poverty for yourself and the people around you?

You are my story, and I am your story. I lived and survived the chaos.

Healing only came after learning of God's love for me—not just the salvation but also the purpose and value that God gives to overcome the emotional scars of abuse. He created each one of us for a divine purpose.

Domestic Violence alone will destroy your self-esteem, but in addition, I grew up in Arizona foster care (living in a group home because there are never enough foster homes), only leaving foster care at age eighteen. So, experiencing abuse, rejection, abandonment, and cruelty was deeply rooted and produced deep feelings of loneliness and low-self-esteem.

For years, I believed the words spoken over me as a child that I was stupid, unwanted, and would never have any value.

In my marriage, I was a victim of domestic violence. At times, I lived sixteen miles from the nearest town. After eighteen years, I was able to get to a safe place only then to spend another eighteen months in homelessness trying to get back to Arizona. I slept on bare wooden floors without a blanket or pillow and, for nine months, transitioned between homeless shelters. I used this time to study and observe people. I also studied the differences in successful and struggling shelters and human service programs.

To study a program as a participant on the inside was different. I have a Bachelor Degree in Business from Northern Arizona University and experience in working with nonprofits, writing grants and policies, creating human service programs, serving on community boards, supervising and training case managers in state offices, and providing workshops for staff and participants.

I was intrigued in observing how some shelters seemed to be successful in delivering services and other organizations or shelters struggled. What was making the great shelters great? How were they organized?

What made the difference? Why were some participants making progress and others stuck? Why did I beat the odds and graduate from college? When only 3 percent of kids who age out of foster care ever graduate from college (More foster kids start college but do not graduate.) Why do many shelter participants return to abuse?

Who are we? A summation of our life experiences, the place we were born, the age or sex we are, the family we came from, a mother, father, sister, brother, child? What are we junk, somewhat good and bad, humans, kings and priest?

What is *our* image of God? What is our image of our self or others? Who is God and what does He say about us? We are created in His image, so who are we? We are a treasure to be found, a treasure to give, a pearl that is sought after by the seeker and redeemed for a rich price.

First, God is our Lord, King, master, ruler, rightly judging, fair, father, leader, comforter, brother, friend, lover, creator, all-knowing, holy, transparent, wise and leader, protector, teacher, lovely, beautiful, provider, transforming, potter—*the I Am*!

At age five, my grandmother used to take me to church. This planted a seed, and I accepted Jesus as my savior at this young age. After becoming an adult, I got out of the negative cycle by growing in God. It took many years, learning through my mistakes and about God's value for me and how He saw me. It took time to break the negatives and lies spoken over me all my life, the ones that told me I was not wanted and had no value. He sees all of us as extremely valuable. It was not His plan for any of us to be hurt, and He wants to take the hurt and replace it with His love and healing. He wants to restore us to His original design and purpose. So, I will pursue, fight, and complete what I am to do. I will not let anything stop me! You also are valuable!

I lived the pain of abuse as a child and survived domestic violence. I am *now proof* that God can and will restore.

In the pain came an assignment to bring hope and healing. I was designed for this purpose. God's healing is found in Him. There are many good programs. This is beyond a financial program or support group. The design is to take broken lives, bring freedom, and bring healing, breaking the cycle of emotional or destructive behaviors and chronic poverty. We can all walk away from our purpose. I will not! God told me this book would not be easy to write (and it has not been). Satan would not want this book to come out; therefore, I will push through all the attacks, call on the name of Jesus and my only father God, asking for wisdom, asking for prayer to fight and accomplish this assignment. For Satan has no power unless we give it to Him. There is no spiritual football game. There is only a side that is divine by God, designed for God's purpose, and God has called me into my purpose.

I pray this workbook will open the doors that you may never doubt God's love for you again and receive a lasting healing from your pains or tragedy in life. You also have been called for a purpose.

There is very little about my story in this book—just enough to let you know the cycle of abuse and poverty can be broken. This workbook is here to help you find your victory story and victory voice! Our promises come from the word of God, for you are loved.

God does love you. Yes, He wants and desires you. You are His child. In Song of Solomon 7:10 (KVJ), it is written, "I am my beloved and His desire is for me." He desires you even more than you can imagine. He wants to be your healer, your safe father. If you allow Him, He can come into your pain and give you peace. Ask Him now to start the healing. He will hear you.

God is a father.

I am a daddy's girl. Some say, "Don't reduce God to such a low point." I say and have learned that if you need a "father," He is a father to the fatherless.

> A father of the fatherless and a judge for the widows, Is God in His holy habitation. (Psalm 68:5, NASB)

He is a comforter to the brokenhearted and hurting.

> The Lord is near to the brokenhearted, and saves those who are crushed in spirit. (Psalm 34:18, NASB)

I have a heavenly Father. I have a wonderful, powerful God who can create all things. With just a word spoken, He started the world to spinning. And yes, in my finite mind, I know He can catch one of the stars He named and release it back to its place in the universe. I imagine Him that big, but He is bigger even than I can imagine.

> He counts the number of the stars;
> He gives names to all of them. (Psalm 147:4, NASB)

Welcome to this workbook, a place where we will explore God and His abundance of mercy, goodness, healing, and love.

> Surely goodness and lovingkindness
> will follow me all the days of my life, and
> I will dwell in the house of the Lord forever. (Psalm 23:6, NASB)

CHAPTER 1

How Big Is Your God?

As little children, some of us were allowed to play outside when it was dark or at sunset. One of our experiences or enjoyments may have been to catch fireflies (or lighting bugs). We would watch the little creatures flash their lights around us and try to catch them. We could let them land on our hand and fly away or keep them in a jar or let them flash freely in our room at night. Sometimes, we made rings and necklaces or painted our hands and faces from the glow of the little bug's light source.

Your childhood experiences may not have included lighting bugs but did include some other enjoyment or interest you found in your surroundings. Reflect on your memory as you think about God's possibilities in that memory. Did you see butterflies, frogs, moss on a tree, raindrops on a window, a water puddle, or an insect in a room where you were kept and could not escape?

How big is God?

In the same way that we may have played with fireflies, hold them and release them. How big is God? Does He enjoy

His creations? What can or might God do with the stars He named and created?

> He (God) determines the number
> of the stars and calls them all by name.
> (Psalm 147:4, NIV)

Have you ever thought that He could, at any time, call any one of the billions of stars by name and have it come to Him? Could not God reach out His arm and have the star land on His hand or shoulder? Couldn't God enjoy the star as it twists and sparkles, with the radiating glow dripping down and through His fingers? Would God not be able to watch the massive star that He named and created dance in the palm of His hand or in His throne room? Just like we may have enjoyed chasing fireflies, watching them light up in our hand as children, could not God enjoy the star's creation and power? And then sending the star back to complete the original purpose He created it for, to fulfill a divine purpose in a perfect location and assigned place, positioned with the billions of other stars He created and named.

> Great is our Lord, and mighty in
> power; His understanding has no limit.
> (Psalm 147:5, NIV)

In the same way we can see the mighty bolt of lightning flash across and light up a dark sky, would God not be able to catch one of those massive lightning bolts? He could hold it in His grasp, keep it alive with His power, and release it back to its place in the dark atmosphere. The great sound of thunder comes from God's creation of lightning. God is big enough to enjoy His creation. He created the earth, sky, seas, heavens, universe, animals all for us to enjoy with Him. "And God saw all that he had made, and it was very good" (Genesis 1:31a, NASB).

When God created the earth and all the outer universes, He always said, "It is *good*!"

That's how big I can imagine God. But He is even bigger than my finite mind can imagine. He is the one and only God of Holiness. He was here before beginning of time, and He will be here after time is no longer counted. After we have put our watches and cell phones away, God will be here!

Imagine God: Write down what you imagine Him to be.

He created you! He doesn't make mistakes or junk.

> Many are the plans in a man's heart, but it is the Lord's purpose that prevails. (Proverbs 19:21, NIV)

> But I have raised you up for this very purpose, that I might show you my power and that my name might be proclaimed in all the earth. (Exodus 9:16, NIV)

God chose to create the heavens and the earth.

With everything that was created, it was first spoken (His plan) the words to create.

In the beginning, God said, "*Let* there be…and it was so." Each time God then (speaking again) said, "It was good!" Reference Genesis 1, complete chapter (NIV or NASB).

With everything He created, He first spoke out loud the word *let*, setting into action all of creation and His plan. He also never said He made a mistake. God always said that it was good. All His creation was and still is good. He does not make mistakes, and He does not make junk. You also are not a mistake and can never lose His love.

There is only one time during God's creation He did not say, "It is good." When He created us to be like Him and gave us authority over all His creation, He said, "It is *very good!*"

> And God saw all that He had made, and behold, it was very good. And there was evening and there was morning, the sixth day. (Genesis 1:31, NASB)

You were created in God's image. You were also thought of at the beginning of time. When God set the whole plan into creation, speaking the words *"Let there be!"* His words became a command of energy and action, and you, at the beginning of creation, were a part of that plan.

We see God as a finite as we see our self with limits of our timelines. God is not confined to our timelines. When He set out His plan, *"Let there be,"* He saw the whole plan from beginning to end. He saw and planned for you, and He also gave you a free choice. He saw the answer to our good and bad choices. He saw the need to provide His Son, Jesus.

In this workbook, we will explore our image of God and learn how to see ourselves as God sees us. We will ask God to step into our lives in the process of healing. We will discover how He can heal your hurts, your memories, allowing Him to come into the pain and help you deal with the nightmare you may have lived. We will learn to see ourselves through the promises of God. He made us, and His plan for us is good.

> He (God) heals the brokenhearted and binds up their wounds. (Psalm 147:3, NIV)

Who Is God?

He is three parts and yet one, this mighty God who created the world, universe, and us: (1) God the father, (2) God the son, and (3) God the Holy Spirit. All three parts of God were there at the creation.

In the beginning, God created the heavens and the earth, and the earth was without void, and darkness covered the face of the earth. His spirit hovered upon the earth. And He said it was good.

God: "In the beginning *God created* the heavens and the earth" (Genesis 1:1, NIV).

Holy Spirit: "The earth was without form and void and darkness was on the face of the deep. And the *Spirit of God* was hovering over the face of the waters" (Genesis 1:2, NIV).

> There is one body and one Spirit—
> Just as you were called to one hope when you were called—one Lord, one faith,

one baptism; one God and Father of all, who is over all and through all and in all. (Ephesians 4:4, NIV)

Jesus was with God in the beginning:

In the beginning *was the word,* and the word was God, and the Word was with God. He was with God in the beginning. (John 1:1, NIV)

And the *Word became flesh and made his dwelling among us.* We have seen his glory, the glory of the One and Only, who came from the Father, full of grace and truth. (John 1:14, NIV)

If you are having trouble seeing God as three parts yet one, try thinking of an egg. It is three parts: a shell, white, and yoke. Each part of an egg serves a different purpose, protecting, supporting, and giving life, but also it is one.

On the following page answer the questions. There is no right or wrong answer. The purpose is to help you think about and explore where you are and look at your true image of yourself and how you now believe about God. Be honest with yourself. God wants to start the healing where you are now. He cannot start with the person you would like to be. You are always a work in progress, but the work is not yet done. Your whole life will always be on the journey to know God.

Questions to Be Answered

When I think of God, I think in His view of me, He is:

Angry	1 2 3 4 5 6 7 8 9 10	Not angry
Unfair	1 2 3 4 5 6 7 8 9 10	Fair
Vengeful	1 2 3 4 5 6 7 8 9 10	Forgiving
Punishing me	1 2 3 4 5 6 7 8 9 10	Forgives me
Selfish	1 2 3 4 5 6 7 8 9 10	Cares about me
Unable to help me	1 2 3 4 5 6 7 8 9 10	Can help me
Doesn't love me	1 2 3 4 5 6 7 8 9 10	Does love me
Unable to love me	1 2 3 4 5 6 7 8 9 10	Can love me
Loves others more than me	1 2 3 4 5 6 7 8 9 10	Loves me the same
Has favorites	1 2 3 4 5 6 7 8 9 10	Wants to help me
Treats some better	1 2 3 4 5 6 7 8 9 10	Treats all equal
Doesn't protect me	1 2 3 4 5 6 7 8 9 10	Can protect me
Is mad at me	1 2 3 4 5 6 7 8 9 10	Is not mad at me
Knows I am a failure	1 2 3 4 5 6 7 8 9 10	Can help me succeed
Made a mistake making me	1 2 3 4 5 6 7 8 9 10	Made me for a reason
He is reason I am this way	1 2 3 4 5 6 7 8 9 10	My actions made this
He is reason this happened	1 2 3 4 5 6 7 8 9 10	Someone else, I chose
I can only expect bad	1 2 3 4 5 6 7 8 9 10	Things can get better
He can't change my life	1 2 3 4 5 6 7 8 9 10	He wants to help bring change
Didn't create me for good	1 2 3 4 5 6 7 8 9 10	My future can be better
I'm own my own	1 2 3 4 5 6 7 8 9 10	God sees everything
Changes His mind	1 2 3 4 5 6 7 8 9 10	Keeps His promises
I don't know who God is	1 2 3 4 5 6 7 8 9 10	I may know God someday

CHAPTER 2

When the World Peels You Like a Banana

God does not make mistakes and He chose to make you. Not only were you His choice, He placed you on earth at a particular time in His plan. You could have been born into the time of Renaissances, at the time of the Roman Empire, when horse and buggies were still being used, or you could have been born to walk the earth on foot with Abraham, King David, Ruth, or Esther. These Bible men and women had a purpose to fulfill at a particular time and place. You have a purpose to fulfill within the time that you were born.

> Before I formed you in the womb,
> I knew you, before you were born, I set
> you apart. (Jeremiah 1:5a, NASB)

You were seen before you were born. We are all born into a cursed world. Some of us were born into harder circumstances. These hard places were not by God's original choice, but because as humans, man has a freewill to change the direction of life for themselves or personal family, friends, or even strangers. God is still in control of the outcome and can reposition and restore you to fulfill the Godly purpose for which you were created.

> For it is God who works in you to will and to act according to his GOOD purpose. (Philippians 2:13, NIV)

> For everyone looks out for his own interest, not those in Jesus Christ. (Philippians 2:21, NIV)

If you were born into chaos, remember God can bring you out of the chaos. If you feel like you are in mud soup or a family of blood soup, and you have been violated at a young age, God did not plan for that to happen to you. God never designed you to be hurt.

> But whoever causes one of these little ones who believe in Me to stumble (sin), it is better for him to have a heavy millstone be hung around his neck, and that he be drowned in the depth of the sea. Woe to the world because of its stumbling blocks! For it is inevitable that stumbling blocks come; but woe to that man through whom the stumbling blocks come! (Matthew 18:6–7, NASB)

It was not His original plan. God did not create man to fall and make a mess of the world. Because man has fallen, He provided a way out of our chaos. Today also, He does not abandon you in your life circumstances. Even when you have felt abandoned, God did not abandon you. God's desire is for you to have an abundant life. Let's look at your dream world that you would have liked to be born into. Write down what your childhood (adulthood) world looks like if you had a choice.

Dream Big!

1)
2)
3)

God does not make mistakes but man does.
God is all present but does not interfere with our choices. We must ask Him to participate in our life or someone must ask or pray on our behalf. Note: Your personal decision to ask Jesus to be your savior is a request only you can make for you.

> Jesus looked at them and said, 'With man this is impossible, but with God all things are possible." (Matthew 19:26, NIV)

In your dream life, there will be some things that are possible now, and there are other things that may not be possible now but someday can become possible. Write down three things that, with God's help, may become possible now or in the near future (examples: being safe, nice place to live, good food, great vacation, exciting new job):

1)
2)
3)

> For it is God who is at work in you, both to will and work for His good pleasure. (Philippians 2:13, NASB)

> But He said, 'The things impossible with men are possible with God." (Luke 18:27, NASB)

When will the nightmare end?
God did not create man to fall and make a mess of the world. It was not His original plan. When man does fall, He provided a way out of our chaos.

He (God) saw the fall from Eden and the need to provide His son. He is the God of many chances but also a just and true God.

> The Rock! His works is perfect, for all his ways are just; A God of faithfulness and without injustice, righteous and upright is He. (Deuteronomy 32:4, NASB)

You may have lived in the nightmare for years and experienced trauma many times. The nightmare may have happened one time but has destroyed your peace. Any memories of trauma time are often painful. He is here now to help you heal. Invite Him into the memory. Ask Him to show you where to start. You may have asked God to rescue you. You may have felt abandoned and that God did not answer. Ask again, God is listening. Because of the pain, God sometimes takes us through the healing in small steps.

God is grieving over you when you are hurting. Ask Him to start to bring you His peace, heal the pain, the scars of the body, and the scars of the emotions, memory, and your mind. He wants to heal the trigger-scars planted deep (thoughts that bring you back in memory, to reliving the event, emotions, abuse, or pain).

You may not feel an instant change, but ask. The pain from the hurt that came over years of abuse or neglect may take a while. The pain that happened over time may be extreme.

> "Because he loves me," says the Lord, "I will rescue him; I will protect him, for he acknowledges my name. He will call upon me, and I will answer him; I will be with him in trouble, I will deliver him and honor him. With long life I will satisfy him and show him my salvation. (Psalm 91:14–16, NIV)

God in His wisdom may choose to take you through the healing process in smaller steps. He loves you and knows how to nurture, comfort, and restore you, holding you closely, while bringing you through His complete healing with the least amount of pain. The healing process can be painful. The pain does go away. If you choose to stay in the hurt and brokenness, the pain you experience now will never go away, and additional pains will be layered from new living. In choosing to live where you are at in the pain, then *all* pain will become more intense and magnified. Choose to be healed.

> Who is the man who fears the Lord?
> He will instruct him the way he should choose. His soul will abide in prosperity, and his descendants will inherit the land.

> The secret of the Lord is for those who fear Him, and He will make them know his covenant, my eyes are continually toward the Lord, For He will pluck my feet out of the net. (Psalm 25:12, NASB)

> This is what the Lord says-your Redeemer, the Holy One of Israel "I am the Lord your God, who teaches you what is best for you, who directs you in the way you should go." (Isaiah 48:17, NIV)

He desires to bring you into peace, strength, and joy. Ask Him to make you whole and healthy in Him. He wants to be your protector, provider, completely healing and restoring you. Ask Him to give you courage and heal your deepest hurts. (It does take courage to go through some of the healing process.)

> For God has not given us a spirit of fear, but of power and of love and of a sound mind. (2 Timothy 1:7, NKJV)

During the process of healing, it is natural to feel the pain more deeply sometimes. The sea may be calm in your life, and suddenly, a big wave crashes you into the shore or you find yourself deep underwater again being slammed against the sharp rocks. There may be a trigger that reopens a wound. As you are healed, believe that any setbacks will become less frequent and less severe. Learn from a setback that may have caused pain. Don't overthink it, but is God doing some more healing? Why did that hurt so much? Were you able to overcome the pain faster? Or are you no longer noticing turbulence and living in peace?

Invite God into your healing process. Ask for His help. God wants to bring you through and may be gentle or more direct at times. The pain did not happen overnight. Give God time in His wisdom to bring you into total healing, restored for your original purpose.

> Immediately the boy's father explained, "I do believe; help me overcome my unbelief." (Mark 9:24, NIV)

> Now it is God who has made us for this very purpose and given us the Spirit as a deposit, guaranteeing what is to come. We live by faith not by sight. (2 Corinthians 5:5, 7; NIV)

Be open to God's healing and supernatural power. God always can, and will at times, bring an instant healing and miracle release.

> Heal me O Lord, and I will be healed; Save me and I will be saved, For thou art my praise. (Jeremiah 17:14, NASB)

Can you forgive the person or persons who hurt you?
Yes.   No.   Not yet.   I am working on it.

1) Forgiving does not mean making excuses for someone's bad behavior!
2) Forgiving does not mean that you must let the person back into your life!

We can forgive and recognize that the relationship is not safe. We may no longer be able to have a relationship with someone who may have hurt us (or our family) in the past and will be dangerous for us to continue to be around.

> If it is possible, as far as it depends on you, live at peace with everyone. Do not take revenge, my friends, but leave room for God's wrath, for it is written: "It is mine to avenge; I will repay," says the Lord. (Romans 12:18–19, NIV)

> Be kind and compassionate to one another, forgiving each other, just as in Christ God forgave you. (Ephesians 4:32, NIV)

Write down the names of whom you need to forgive:

_____

Forgiving is a part of the healing and is a heart choice. Our emotions or thoughts may not yet be in line with the choice to forgive. Forgiving may also start with a verbal choice to forgive—saying out loud to yourself or someone (you feel is safe and can be trusted with personal information). I forgive the person who hurt me. With God, you are still working out the process in the heart. First step, deciding to forgive.

Let God into your pain. Healing of the pain may take time and be a process. God knows how much pain you are in, and He knows how to bring you safely through the process into total healing. (God is wise and heals without overwhelming you.) You were a victim, but *you are no longer a victim*. That was the old you, and you are becoming new in Christ.

Learning about and *focusing* on who God says you are and the good He wants for your life will help. His purpose for you is a good purpose.

> For he says, "In the time of my favor I heard you, and in the day of salvation I helped you. I tell you, now is the time of God's favor, now is the day of salvation. (2 Corinthians 6:2, NIV)

Reading and saying scriptures out loud about how valuable you are helps you overcome the negatives you have heard and believed. Learn who God says you are, how He sees you. Reviewing His promises to you and His writings about you will help you overcome the past broken record of negative images. Believe the promises that you are a loved, chosen, a valued person with a purpose to complete. Our job is to discover God's love. Replacing the lie that we are broken comes by hearing and knowing that God loves us and wants to heal our broken, painful lives and bring us to His loving care. Letting you crawl, as a child, into His lap and know the love of a *good* and *pure* father.

> He heals the brokenhearted and binds up their wounds. (Psalm 147:3, NIV)

> Rejoice in the Lord always. I will say it again: Rejoice! Let your gentleness be evident to all. The Lord is near. (Philippians 4:4–9, NIV)

> Being confident of this, that he who began a good work in you will carry it on to completion until the day of Christ Jesus. (Philippians 1:6, NIV)

Assignment

Using your Bible, look up the *promise scriptures* (find the verses and reference). Sometimes only a part of scripture is given, and you want to find the reference scripture and write out the whole text and Bible location where you find the text. Other times, the text reference is given, you will locate the verse, and copy the verse into your assignment. You may have a dictionary or concordance in your Bible that can help you look up the scripture. There are telephone applications such as: Biblegateway.com and other phone tools that can help you find the scriptures. The purpose of this assignment is to become more familiar with tools that will help you grow in Christ and seeing yourself as He sees you—wonderfully made and loved by Him. Learning a new tool can help you encourage yourself in God's love. His love is always available when you are alone or need Him. Meditating on God's promises will start to replace any negative image that you have heard and believe.

Questions

When have you felt abandoned or alone?

What promise scripture can you find?

Example: Find the reference for this scripture fragment:

"I will never leave you or forsake you…"

Do you believe God meant for you to be hurt? *Why or why not?*
What promise scripture can you find?

"I know the plans I have for you to prosper you…"

Do you believe it is your fault or you deserved it?
What promise scripture can you find?

"For we all have come short of the glory of God."

Have you ever felt like hurting yourself to end the pain?
Do you know who is safe to call when you feel this pain?

Where was god in all of this?

> But you are a shield around me, O Lord;
> You bestow glory on me and lift my head.
> To the Lord I cry aloud,
> And He answers me from his holy hill
> I lie down and sleep:
> I wake again, because the Lord sustains me. (Psalm 3:3–5, NIV)

Can God heal the pain of abuse or abandonment?

> He heals the brokenhearted and binds up their wounds. (Psalm 147:3, NIV)

Christ *as* comforter: Look up and write down 2 Corinthians 1:3–8.

Does God love you?

> For God so loved the world that he gave his one and only Son, that whosoever believes in him shall not perish but have eternal life

Find the scripture mentioned above.

Are you a mistake? (Find the two different scriptures: finish the quote and reverence.)

> "I will be a Father to you, and you will be my sons and daughters."

What scripture?

> "For God did not send his son into the world to condemn the world."

What scripture?

Does God have a plan for you?

> Now it is God who has made us for this very purpose and has given us the Spirit as a deposit, guaranteeing what is to come. (2 Corinthians 5:5, NIV)

Find and write out the following scripture and its location:

> "For I know the plans I have for you…"

Is God punishing you?

> "Whoever believes in him is not condemned, but whoever does not believe stands condemned already because he has not believed in the name of God's one and only Son."

What is the scripture?

How big is God?
Does He have the power, and can He help you?

> "In him we were also chosen, having been predestined according to the plan of him

> who works out everything in conformity with the purpose of his will."

What is the scripture?

Does God want a better life for you?

> And the God of all grace, who called you to his eternal glory in Christ, after you have suffered a little while, will himself restore you and make you strong, firm and steadfast. To him be the power for ever and ever. Amen. (1 Peter 5:10–11, NIV)

Find:

> "And you also were included in Christ when you heard the word of truth the gospel of your salvation. Having believed you were marked in him with a seal of the promised Holy Spirit, who is the deposit guaranteeing our inheritance."

What is the scripture?

He will help you heal when you let God into the pain.

Discuss and explore with your group who God is. What scriptures support the goodness of God and how He views you? Did you or your group discover any other scripture promises that you can use?

Explore Who God Is

He's a teacher—learn of His love, acceptance, provision, peace, lessons, direction, leadership, who you are in the I Am of Him. Realize that God does not make junk. He does not make mistakes; He made me, and He made you for a purpose. You will learn in this book who you are, how your experiences, no matter how chaotically, skewed, off beat, tragic, and rocky you started, you still have a purpose, a divine destiny, and direction that's been placed on you. You can find the place of healing and bring healing to others and point them to God.

All your life you never stop learning. Writing down the promises of God and who He says you are will give you a place to go to review. A quick reminder of who you are in God when negative or old habits try to intrude your thoughts. Meditate on God's image of you, and memorize God's word and promise.

Look up, and write down Joshua 1:8.

> When I remember you on my bed, I mediate on You in the night watches. (Psalm 63:6, NASB)

> I will remember my song in the night; I will mediate with my heart, and my spirit ponders. (Psalm 77:6, NASB)

> Make me understand the way of Your precepts, So I will mediate on Your wonders. (Psalm 119:27, NASB)

> I'm feeling terrible—I couldn't feel worse! Get me on my feet again. You promised, remember? When I told my story, you responded; train me well in your deep wisdom. Help me understand these things inside and out so I can ponder your miracles wonders. My sad life's dilapidated, a falling-down barn; build me up again by your Word. Barricade to road that goes Nowhere; grace me with your clear revelation. I choose the true road to Somewhere, I post your road signs at every curve and corner. I grasp and cling to whatever you tell me; God, don't let me down! I'll run the course you lay out for me if you'll just show me how. (Psalm 119:25–32, MSG)

Healing Takes Time

When you are at your lowest low, when you would rather die because you think it hurts too much to live, when you have been violated physically, emotionally, mentally, God was there, and He saw you hurting. He could not rescue you because He cannot violate choices of our freewill. (It may have been someone else's freewill that violated you.) The pain and hurting are not the plan He had for you. He is here to make it right and restore you to the original purpose of safety and goodness in your life and family. Because you have a choice, you can choose to let the healing begin. He will help you heal when you let God see your pain.

You may never know why. The healing may take time, as you were damaged over many years. (Even if the event was only once, it played out in your memories over many years.) Ask how you can now be made whole in Christ Jesus, in the Father, and how you can now be so whole and healthy that out of your pain can someday minister to others. Allow God to heal you. (It starts with a choice.) Allow Him to walk you back through the pain. Allow yourself to see Him running to help you and loving you in a perfect way and bringing you to the other side of the pain.

Write down or draw a picture of God running to help you. How does it feel?

As you see God wanting to help you, allow yourself to release the pain of the abuse you went through. Give Him the pain. *The pain and memories may have become the biggest part of your identity.* You may only see yourself through the event that happened to you. You may see yourself as battered, broken, used, ugly, no longer able to accept and see yourself in any other way but through the vision of the abuse. You may feel rejected; not only do you believe others reject you, but you have also learned to reject yourself. It may be hard or take a few attempts to give the pain to God. Why? Because it is a big part of your life. It carries emotions and scars.

It may have scarred your life at a very early age. You may know that you were never wanted. How do you deal with that kind of rejection?

He wants to take your pain! He is big enough. He has already taken your pain to the cross when He died for you. You must also be willing to surrender the pain to Him.

Find a scripture that says God is the comforter.

Blank space is sometimes found at the end of a lessons. Use the space to write down what God may be telling you.

CHAPTER 3

Is Your Tortoise Shell Too Small?

God desires to give you a new shell. He wants to replace your old tortoise shell that is too small and heavy. Your old shell reflects too many battle scars and is tattooed with bad memories. You are still growing in the knowledge of God's love for you. Part of growing is learning to trust that God loves you. He is leading and directing. He does want good for you, and He is fair. When He makes a decision to replace your old shell and lead you into safety, He is looking at the better route and plans the best outcome for success. He sees beyond what you can see.

> And he said, "The Lord is my rock and my fortress and my deliverer; my God, my rock in who I take refuge; my shield and the horn of my salvation, my stronghold and my refuge; my savior thou dost save me from violence." (2 Samuel 22:2–3, NASB)

You may already know that your current situation (tortoise shell) no longer meets your needs. It does take faith and courage to let go of the old. Are you willing and ready to let God do the leading? Is it God's time to give you a new shell? Have you grown enough, gained enough ground, found yourself struggling upside down in your current shell trying to do life your way with no skills to turn right side up again and are ready for God's intervention?

A tortoise (or turtle) learns to navigate in a small environment from the low ground. It spends the days searching to eat only the vegetation in the immediate area. If it stays at ground level, it has limited resources and can easily get into trouble. When attempting to climb higher, it may fall. The shell of the tortoise is designed to fulfill one purpose. Only when it is upright can it be used for protection. This same protective shell becomes deadly when the turtle is upside down. After a fall that lands the tortoise on the back and out of position, it struggles with strong feet and sharp toenails to gain traction in the soil, desperate to turn back over. If it stays out of alignment for the purpose of the design of the shell, the same heavy armor is a death trap leading to starvation, dehydration, and attacks from predators.

Have you outgrown your tortoise shell?

In this chapter, we will look at our tortoise shell. There will be a lot of questions to think about. This is a chapter for honest self-assessment. Looking at where you are starting from today is necessary before changes can be made for the better life. Looking at the honest self gives us opportunity to see progress and God moving in our healing.

A tortoise has limited skills, and unlike the tortoise, we need to develop greater skills that will keep us alive and move us into our destiny. You will explore skills to turn right side up again: Do you know how to seek God to right yourself? Do you recognize when you need to ask for help, and do you know how to ask? Is help available when you need it, and do you have a support system you can trust?

With new resources and skill(s), you will be able to turn right side up again and gain traction. You may find that you are not called to be a turtle with a limited view, but instead, you are learning to be an eagle able to explore the abundance of resources, expanding your territories, with no boundaries to stop you from gaining all God has for you in His beautiful promises and gifts.

Is your turtle shell too small?

Are you in an environment that keeps you stuck? Currently upside down in your heavy shell looking for ways to turn right side up again? Have you grown enough, gained enough ground, or found yourself lacking the skills to turn right side up again?

What is your skill level? How is God training you for your future? What is your timeline? What is God's timeline? Do the timelines match? Are you comfortable in the pace? Is your tortoise shell (environment) too small? Do you want to move more quickly but find that the shell you are in has been outgrown? Can everyone in your life now go with you? Are you carrying an old shell that has extra baggage? *Your new shell must start with the creator of your shell.*

God is your creator and has given you a unique assignment. How do you learn to seek God to right yourself and discover this assignment?

Start where you are in your current awareness of God. Each day you have the opportunity to learn and grow in your knowledge of God, building on your understanding of God, Jesus, and the Holy Spirit. He is an unlimited, vast God with many qualities that He will reveal to you. We can never stop growing in finding out more about God's character, love, and benefit of being His child, receiving inheritance discovered in His promises. We have so much to learn.

God desires to have a relationship with you. He created you for this relationship as a covenant of love and communion with Him. A covenant is a contract (binding agreement) to be honored and held. It cannot be broken by God. The covenant is between you and God. It allows the holder in the covenant to have privileges and rights to possess and rule over the inheritance that was given.

> God blessed them and said to them, "Be fruitful and increase in number; fill the earth and subdue it. Rule over the fish of the sea and the birds of the air and over every living creature that moves on the ground." (Genesis 1:28, NIV)

> "This is the covenant that I will make with them after that time, says the Lord. I will put My laws in their hearts, and will write them on their minds." Then He adds: "Their sins and lawless acts I will remember not more." (Hebrews 10:16–17, NIV)

God will not break the covenant He has given you. If you are unaware of the covenant and inheritance you have, it does not mean it is not yours. Learning to exercise your rights to the inheritance starts with learning what is in the contract of the covenant. This covenant is like a *legal will*. A will is written to reveal the inheritance and the benefactors at the death of someone. But who died? You are here and surely not dead.

Jesus died so that we may be the benefactors of the promises of God the father.

> Praise be to the God and Father of our Lord Jesus Christ! In his great mercy he has given us new birth into a living hope through the resurrection of Jesus Christ from the dead, and into an inheritance that can never perish, spoil or fade—kept in heaven for you. (1 Peter 1:3–4, NIV)

The first part of the covenant is our right to salvation and have authority. Jesus paid the price for all our sins being crucified on the cross.

> If I told you earthly things and you do not believe, how shall you believe if I tell you heavenly things? (John 3:13, NASB)

> It is you who are the sons of the prophets, and of the covenant which God made with your fathers, saying to Abraham, "And in your seed all the fam-

ilies of the earth shall be blessed." (Acts 3:25, NASB)

Learning of God also includes becoming familiar with the promises He has already given you. His promises are in the Bible, and there are ways to build your understanding of God. When reading or listening to God's word, you grow and replace the negative beliefs with who God sees you as. Choosing translations of the Bible that you are comfortable in reading will help you understand His promises and your rights. If you are comfortable of your resources, you will use them more.

> This book of the law shall not depart from your mouth, but you shall meditate on it day and night, so that you may be careful to do according to all that is written in it; for then you will make your way prosperous, and then you will have success. (Joshua 1:8, NASB)

Find Godly teachers to learn from.

> How blessed is the man who does not walk in the counsel of the wicked, nor stand in the path of sinners, nor sit in the seat of scoffers! But his delight is in the law of the Lord, and in His law (word) he meditates day and night. (Psalm 1:1–2, NASB)

Praying is hard for many who do not know where to start. Prayer is just talking to God and spending time with

Him. He wants to talk with you. He wants to hear your voice. He created you so that you and He can spend time together talking. He understands your language and slang, and He will speak to you in a way that He knows you will understand. He desires to be with you.

> I am my beloved's and his desire is for me. (Song of Solomon 7:10, NASB)

The more you talk to God, the more comfortable you will become with hearing His voice and His heart. He will reveal His plans to help you.

> Our help is in the name of the Lord, who made heaven and earth. (Psalm 124:8, NASB)

> The counsel of the Lord stands forever, the plans of His heart from generation to generation. (Psalm 33:11, NASB)

> In God I have put my trust, I shall not be afraid. What can man do to me? (Psalm 56:11, NASB)

> And again, "I will put My trust in Him," And again, "Behold, I and the children whom God has given Me." (Hebrews 2:13, NASB)

> For every house is built by someone, but the builder of all things is God. (Hebrews 3:4, NASB)

> Call to Me, and I will answer you, and I will tell you great and might things, which you do not know. (Jeremiah 33:3, NASB)

> God's blessings follow you and await you at every turn: when you don't follow advice of those who delight in wicked schemes, when you avoid sin's highway when judgment and sarcasm beckon you, but you refuse. (Psalm 1:1, Voice)

God will bring a support system.

Finding a support system is important in fulfilling your God call. Identify those who may speak into your life with sound leadership.

Do you recognize when you need to ask for help, and do you know how to ask? Is help available when you need it, and do you have a support system you can trust? Where you are lacking a support system, ask God to send trusted supports, and He will send the right mentors.

There are many prayer (telephone) numbers which have people ready to pray with you. Some are the following: your local church, trusted prayer friends, Trinity Broadcasting Network, Family Broadcasting, Daystar, Kenneth Copeland Ministries, Life Outreach International. Radio stations: KLOVE, KFLR, Air1. There are many more places that provide prayer.

Learn also to grow in your own prayer life to pray for yourself and others in need.

Some of your tortoise shell will need to stay.

> The plans of the diligent lead surely to advantage, but everyone who is hasty comes surely to poverty. (Proverbs 24:8, NASB)

Keep in your plan the parts that must stay. (You may need to care for children.) What items on your baggage list do you still need to carry? (Example: You must work but have a goal to go to school or you want to seek a better job.)

What is your skill level? How is God training you for your future? What is your time line?

Are you comfortable in your current pace? Write down when you want to reach the goal.

Using chapter 2: Copy down what your childhood (adulthood) world looks like if you had a choice.

Dream Big!

1)
2)
3)

What are your goals, your dreams, your desire for yourself and those of your past and present? Choose one, and write down your *biggest dream plan.*

I will dream big!

> Commit your works to the Lord and your plans will be established. The mind of man plans his way, but the Lord directs his steps. (Proverbs 16:3,9, NASB)

What are the starting steps to reach your dream?

1)
2)
3)

Are the dreams you have for yourself on track? Do you have a plan? Write down your achievable dream plan.

Within six months, I will accomplish:

Within one year, I will accomplish:

Within two years, I will accomplish:

Where do you have help? (within United States)

> Prepare plans by consultation and make war by wise guidance. (Proverbs 20:18, NASB)

Do you have the strength that must be there to support your plan? Do you know where to start?

Write down resources in your community that may help you reach your plan. Explore job career or advancements.

A good job:

Where do I find career information pages?

What does it pay?

What skills and knowledge do I need to get and keep the dream job?

Is there a similar job or entry job that will lead me to the job I want to have?

What do I know about the job? Why do I want this career?

Schools:

What schools or training are in the community?

What are the requirements for admission?

Can you receive training from other sources?
Are there free training events offered in your area?
What is and how do I use O'NET?
Is *workforce* available in my area?

Write down who may be a support system you can trust. If there is no one at this time, write down the word *none*. This is a place of prayer for God to bring a trusted support system.

Who may be a trusted resource to speak into your life?

Learn to encourage yourself by growing in your knowledge of the word of God. Listening to good Bible teachings, and reading your Bible will bring into your world biblical instruction. Answers to every problem can be found in the Bible.

When asking for help, seek good resources and wise leadership. The book of Proverbs (thirty-one chapters) is written by King David to his people for instruction in wisdom for life. King David made mistakes and later was able to speak into the lives of others. Proverbs is written to introduce *wisdom* as something to be sought.

> I guide you in the way of wisdom and lead you along straight paths. When you walk, your steps will not be hampered; when you run, you will not stumble. Hold on to instruction, do not let it go; guard it well, for it is your life. (Proverbs 4:11–13, NIV)

Life and Your Tortoise Shell

Now look at your life baggage. Beyond God and spiritual needs, what other baggage do you carry?

Write down extra baggage you may carry.

What extra baggage weight is possible to drop?

Make a plan to let go of the extra baggage. Write down your beginning plan—where you can start and the steps that need to be in place to leave extra baggage behind. (Your extra baggage is your tortoise shell, and it should start to change, becoming lighter.)

Is your tortoise shell too small? Do you want to move more quickly but find that the shell you are in has been outgrown? Set time to reach you goal.

Do I have benefits for retraining as a dislocated worker?

Thinking Outside of the Tortoise Shell Box—United States

Would you like to own your own business or work from home? Not every temperament makes them a good candidate to work from home or have their own business. Explore your strength and weakness in self-discipline and time management. Can you be motivated enough to work from home? Do you have an environment that will support working from home?

Where do you do the research and locate a *legitimate* company that lets you work from home?

Some are resources: Better Business Bureau, Attorney General, Researching Company Name: (1) how long have they been in business, (2) are they local, (3) are there complaints against them, (4) does there offer of income seem too good to be real?

What resources are available if you want to start your own business?

- Local community colleges and schools may provide entrepreneur classes (business workshops)
- Small Business Administration (SBA) US Federal Government provides webinars.
- S.C.O.R.E (Service Corps of Retired Executives) provides volunteer mentors to help you start and grow a business.

Are you eligible to receive services from a state case manager such as Vocational Rehabilitation or from the Veteran's Administration? They both offer self-employment assistance.

Libraries may provide books, magazines, and articles about business. *Forbes, Entrepreneur,* and other magazines are found in some libraries.

Books at most libraries are available to help you write a business plans, exploring job markets and trends, leadership, and supervision,

What country are you living, and are there any resources that you can find to help?

Creativity in identifying a problem in the area and solving the problem may be a service you can provide (making clothes for neighbors, using a stick and dirt to teach children how to write or do math, teaching gardening or how to cook with limited food, telling stories of your family history, telling or teaching Bible stories to your community).

Look around you. What do you see? How can you encourage others in your community? What service do you provide or you can provide that will make you feel good or that you love to do? What do you become passionate about, motivates you? This may be a key to your God assignment.

Take Care of Yourself

Are the basics taken care of? Shelter, food, income, transportation? What about friends, support family or no family?

Do friends and family support your goal to rise to a better life? If not, who will support you, and who can you safely talk to about your dreams?

Align with those who also want to have a better life. A tortoise has a low view and does not see beyond a limited area. There is a much larger world to be gained if you look beyond your limited community. You can be the pioneer to leave the chaos, become a leader and mentor for others, leaving behind the struggle of generational poverty or abuse.

If at all possible, try to have someone you can trust to share victory and setbacks, someone who will speak positives into your life, to share the good or small accomplishment as well as help you navigate the hard times, someone who believes in you. This person you should feel safe with to share bad situations without them judging. They recognize that you are just having a bad day and just need to talk about the hurt. They also speak into your life and remind you of your goals and purpose for fighting through the pain and not giving up.

Toxic Relationships

Who is a toxic relationship to your plan? Who does not support, and who do you need to break ties with? Who supports you? If there is no support, a plan can be accomplished on your own, but must you do it all on your own? Ask God to align you with people who are safe and can support your success plan.

It is just as important to be able to share accomplishments, both small and big, with someone who may support your plan. When you have had an exciting event or good day, there is enjoyment in sharing with a trusted person.

Personal testimony: This writer, growing up in foster care and poverty, learned how painful it is to not have anyone to celebrate good or small gains and learning how painful it is to not have a trusted person to share the hard times. The chances of a foster child who turns eighteen while still in the system graduating from a four-year college is only 3 percent. Most older kids in foster live in a group home because there are not enough foster homes. Older children are unlikely to find a permanent home. They called us "throw-away kids." It hurt to not have anyone at a victory, such as graduating from college. It also took longer because I would sabotage my own road to success. Even in college, I still believed I was not worth anything good, believing what I was told as a little girl, "You're stupid, unwanted, a mistake." It took years for God to erase the negatives.

I learned from God that I am valuable.

Coming Back from a Setback

Develop ways to get back on track with your goals. Take a day off and cry, but don't stay in the mud. What tools can you use to help you get back to your success road? Scripture reading, encouraging articles, prayer, participating in a support group that uplifts you.

Also, when you are at your worst days, doubting, and discouraged, there needs to be someone safe who will just listen and let you work through the pain. Always know that you will be able to and want to refocus on your dreams and purpose for your goals. Think about how good it is going to feel when you reach your goal.

Staying Spiritually and Emotionally Healthy

How do you handle anger? Frustration? How do you deal with disappointment? If things do not go your way or have not be completed in the time you want, what scriptures help you?

Write down three or four scriptures that will help you come out of a hard day.

Are you willing to fail? Do you take some risk to learn where you can move forward? When you failed, what did you learn from a failure? Do you try again?

What may be the obstacles to your success plan? What steps will you take to overcome an obstacle?

Failing is not a loss. Failing is a learning tool of how to do it better next time. There may need to be adjustments or new plan. That new job career is not what you wanted anyway. It does not line up with the direction God has told you to go.

Have you learned that your potential to succeed is not a failure unless you quit?

Make plans to reward yourself in little and big successes.

How are you going to reward yourself in little successes?

Example: The volunteer job I just interviewed for went well. Volunteering for this nonprofit is a place I can use my God gifting. I am going to celebrate the good interview and buy myself a soda. I will continue to look for a job that will pay me well.

Self-talk produces good and bad in your life.

Are you your own enemy? Do you sabotage your success with negative self-talk or negative actions?

We all learn how to walk with God. Are you learning to make the right choices? Do you try to use your time wisely? Write down your biggest time-waster. Make a plan that will improve the plan for your success.

Assignment

At the back of the *Burning Fires* workbook are pages to track your time for a week. Tear out the pages, and track your days. If you are meeting with a group, bring the completed pages to the next meeting, *Finding Treasures in Ashes* meeting. If you are working through this workbook on your own, examine your week to see where you may be able to use your time more efficiently. When working alone, it is easier to not make changes that are needed. It will take self-discipline to activate and keep making improvements.

From the assignment, what is your biggest time-waster?

Who hurt you? What do you still believe, the words of the hurt, and what is your behavior from that hurt? Are you still living in it? Does it dictate your actions and thoughts and hinder your success of today?

How can this be changed? What scriptures will help you overcome the hurt? What three scriptures can you write down and memorize to help you heal? Looking at or memorizing (meditating on) promise scriptures of how God sees you will help believe you are whom He says you are. See yourself through His eyes.

We looked at forgiving others who hurt us. Now look at this: Where do you need to forgive yourself? Be honest. Did something happen that was out of your control but you blame yourself? Even if it was not your fault, you may be unforgiving, feel guilty, and blaming yourself. You know God is forgiving, but you haven't forgiven yourself. You're not quite 100 percent sure you are worthy of God's forgiveness. You may or may not have caused a chaos, but you are feeling responsible for the hurt and trauma that happened.

God forgave you!

Write down where you may need to forgive yourself.

Is forgiving yourself hard?
What would happen if you forgave yourself?
What would happen if you forgave someone else?
Does that mean you have to let the person who hurt you back in your life?
What is a safety net? Who can you call that is safe?

1) Will not tell your business.
2) Keeps supporting you in good and bad (your safe person).
3) Holds you accountable to grow.
4) Does not use you.
5) Whom you can also support.

Who may be an unhealthy relationship?

1) Who should no longer be in your life?
2) Are you ready to let them go?

You are stronger than you believe, and God will help you do the rest.

What negative memories are you holding unto? Make plans to let them go and replace them with the way God sees you.

Do negative memories stop you from moving ahead with plans for a better life? Set solid new goals with a time to complete. Finish what you start.

Write down what God is telling you:

CHAPTER 4

Faith Is Like Planting a Carrot, You Can't Keep Pulling It Up by the Roots to See How It's Growing

What you focus on today will produce not only in today but also creates your tomorrow.

> For God is not unjust so as to forget your work and the love which you have shown toward His name, in having ministered and in still ministering to the saints. And we desire that each one of you show the same diligence so as to realize the full assurance of hop until the end. (Hebrews 6:10–11, NASB)

Habits that are negative produce negative results; positive habits produce positive results. Every action taken today is a seed that produces today or reproduces in the future. Both destructive seeds and good seeds produce. Some seeds take longer to produce. Seeds can be related to faith.

When you plant a carrot, you can't keep pulling it up by the roots to see how it is growing. You want your carrot to grow strong, fat, orange, and long into the ground. A carrot is a root, and you can only see the little green top as it grows. It takes faith to believe that something is happening underground. If you pull a root plant, it cannot be replanted without damaging or killing the production of the root.

> Now faith is the substance of things
> hoped for the evidence of things not seen.
> (Hebrews 11:1, KJV)

A hope is just a dream; it is not faith. Many people hope for things, believing that things will change, maybe they will win the lottery, get out of poverty or abuse someday.

Hope is just a dream. Look again at the scripture: "Now faith is the substance of things hoped for the evidence of things not seen." Substance is found in faith. Faith acts. I have faith that Jesus was sent; I have faith that God will provide a way.

Faith also was seen in many people, and their names were listed as people who had faith. This included a prostitute. In faith, some made plans and followed plans of God. Some were told to leave their family behind because the family was not willing to follow the same plan. Some needed to leave others behind because God was calling the others in a different direction so they could fulfill their purpose. Not everyone has the same assignment. Some may be destined to minister to children, others to seniors, or to the homeless.

Whatever your desires, you will find it defined more in detail as you continue to pursue the purpose God has called you to follow. Any plan will not be revealed all at once. We may make a blueprint to look in the direction that we think we should go, but we will not have the whole plan.

God Has Plans for You

A blueprint can be given to many people in part. The electric, plumbing, foundation, landscape, windows, and heating and air system may be given to individual contractors, but only the creator of the plan may have the master plan. In the master's plan, in His vision, is the final outcome. We may only have part of the vision of the plan but are all working toward the final product.

In building, there is a term call the plum line. This tool is to keep the building strait. The Leaning Tower of Pisa, found in Italy, is leaning more each year. The tilt was caused at its construction and foundation.

Building a proper foundation means being patient and using the right mixture of cement, digging deep enough in the ground, and providing supports with the right metal rebars and pillars. Using shortcuts will cause a collapse of the building. The environment also must be correct. When conditions are too wet, too hot, and too cold, the product will fail and can cause a collapse. A finished building with structure damage may be reinforced at great expense and may never be saved.

In an original building plan or remodel, scaffold during construction may not be pretty but is necessary and is only removed when the building can stand on its own.

> His ways prosper at all times; Thy judgements are on high, out of his sight; out of all his adversaries he snorts at them. (Psalm 10:5, NASB)

> For it is God who is at work in you, both to will and to work for His good pleasure. (Philippians 2:13, NASB)

> Behold, I am the Lord, the God of all flesh; is anything too difficult for Me? (Jeremiah 32:27, NASB)

> Ah Lord God! Behold, thou hast made the heavens and the earth by Thy great power and by Thine outstretched arm! Nothing is too difficult for thee. (Jeremiah 32:17, NASB)

Do not regret the foundation and slow process that God is taking you through to make you complete. He holds the master plan. It is only the master who can take your through roads and detours. A pothole in your life is a pain God will smooth and turn into something beautiful. Remember, He never meant for you to go through the emotional and physical pain. By human choice, rather our own choice or someone inflicting pain on us, we suffered hardship, loss, and pain. Only God can take that broken plan and now turn the pain into something that can be used for His kingdom. You may be the one who can reach a person who is today suffering what you suffer through yesterday. When God breaks through with His healing, you can help others. He is creating a road map in you for others to successfully follow.

> Consider it all joy my brethren, when you encounter various trials, knowing that the testing of your faith produces endurance. And let endurance have its perfect result so that you may be perfect and complete, lacking in nothing. (James 1:2–4, NASB)

> Behold I will bring to it health and healing, and I will heal them; and I will reveal to them an abundance of peace and truth. (Jeremiah 33:6, NASB)

If we are not healed yourself, you can become reinjured, and even your pain of not being fully healed may do more damage to you or others. Healing is individual, and the time to heal is individual. It can't be rushed because only God knows all the steps until we are ready to fully reach others. You may be able to help on a short term or smaller basis as you are being healed from you own hurts. This is a growth time to help prepare you for your matured calling.

You are not alone if you struggle with wanting to give up, lose heart, and get discouraged.

> For I know the plans that I have for you, declares the Lord, plans for welfare and not for calamity to give you a future and a hope. (Jeremiah 29:11, NASB)

Assignment

When you plant a carrot, you can't keep pulling it up by the roots to see how it is growing. You may go to the garden and look at the plant to see only that it is still growing. The little hat of green on the carrot is also your little hat of green as a reminder. When you want to move to fast, you may think of your green hat as your dreams of reaching your full potential or belief for something better; it is still a faith work in progress. And the plans God has for you are plans like a carrot growing. You will know when to pull the carrot.

It also takes faith to believe God has a good plan for you. He created you and the universe. You are a part of God's master plan for today.

Prepare the Soil

Search for the right place to plant your carrots. Pick the plot that you are comfortable staying with and investing your time and efforts.

What are you believing for? A new job, house, car, birth of a child, these are your carrots.

Look at your negative habits. What steps are needed to improve?

Water your seeds; provide the right environment to grow.

1) Meditate on the scripture promises that remind you of your seed.
2) God's word says we have the mind of Christ. Look up and write down the scripture.
3) Worship music, listening to messages, attending church, watch tapes.

It is important to take care of the carrots in your garden, or they will die.

Keep the weeds out that will steal light and vitamins from the carrot:

1) Negative and naysayers.
2) It is not necessary to share with everyone; they may speak doubt into what you are believing.

The garden is a witness to others as they pass by. As your seed produces and you pull the carrots, your life becomes a witness of God's promises to others. It is evidence of God's goodness.

> Surely your goodness and love will follow me all the days of my life, and I will dwell in the house of the Lord forever. (Psalm 23:6, NIV)

Don't worry about your seed. You have determined what seeds you wanted to produce when considering your soil. Don't stomp on the garden or abandon it. Someone else may be planting a different garden. That is the calling and talents God gave them to plant.

> Do not be anxious about anything, but in every situation, by prayer and petition, with thanksgiving, present your request to God. (Philippians 4:6, NIV)

Protect it from predators who want to steal your seed and kill the leaf. Predators also can be underground doing damage to your seed. You may work in someone's garden for a time to learn how to garden but someday have your own garden. Fruit will come from the garden.

1) When your life starts producing seed, predators may appear.
2) Jealousy: someone starts gossip and lies.
3) People want your attention and are needy. Time wasters.

Protect your time and your visions and goals. Help at times and allow others to discover and grow in their faith. Being the only resource for someone stunts their growth.

Distractions take you out of focus with the God plan in you. Distraction may disguise as counterfeiting opportunities. The enemy likes to get your attention and stop your seeds from producing. He will try to stop your success. He will try to make you abandon your garden seeds to take care of the weeds in someone else's garden and steal your produce.

God is the resource for other people. He has a purpose for their life, and they can choose to discover that purpose or stay in mediocracy or the chaos.

Those around you will learn more by your example when you follow God's plan and fulfill the purposes He called you to do.

It becomes fun to seek out and discover God's purposes for you.

Choose not to do anything for someone who can do the same thing for themselves.

Others may not want you to succeed. You may hear someone say, "You think your better than us." Or you don't deserve it; stay poor in spirit and things. We have always lived this way.

> Now to him who is able to do immeasurably more than all we ask or imagine, according to his power that is at work within us, to him be glory in the church and in Christ Jesus throughout all generations, for ever and ever! Amen. (Ephesians 3:20–21, NIV)

If you were to plant a carrot seed, what would be the results? Will you pull it up by the roots to see how it is growing? It can't be done. Some seeds take time. I will plant a carrot seed and give it time. It may take longer than I want. But I want my carrot to get long and strong and fat and bright orange. Only the little top I see, and I know it is still growing. I can't keep pulling it up to see how it is growing.

Faith is the substance of things hope for, the evidence of things not seen. Faith is the *substance* of hope; hope is not the driving force. Hope is for things that you cannot see. My carrot is in the ground, and it's only the little top I see. I do not see the evidence of how big the carrot is growing; the evidence is only in the little green top. But I still wait.

If you ask someone what they would like to accomplish, are those their life desires and dreams and goals, many times the response is, "Someday I want to," or "I hope to have." Hoping will not move you forward. What is the plan to apply the hope? When there is not a solid plan for "your hope," it is just a nice thought or saying. Hope has *no* action behind it: Faith has action that is the substance to the hope.

Look at the scripture again, "Now faith is the assurance of things hoped for the conviction things not seen" (Hebrews 11:1, NASB).

1) Now faith—current, in this time (received already as happened in your thoughts)
2) Assurance—knowing it has been done
3) Things—focus of the faith
4) Hoped for—desired becomes alive
5) Conviction—not moving from
6) Things not seen—natural is not the real of already received in the spirit

What are you believing God for now and not just hoping to receive?

How are you applying your faith? What seeds are you planting? What actions are you taking to make your plan a reality? God will water the seeds He gave us to plant if we will put them in the ground. This applies to money seeds of tithes and offering (Malachi 3) or action seeds. Are you looking for work, taking a class, networking, doing an application for apartments or a house? Have you explored resources to buy a house, grants, or school grants? Are your networking, researching, reading, teaching yourself new skill, updating contacts?

Seeds that produce overnight may not be seeds or plants of quality. For example: You can produce a weed overnight and have a result. The weed is there for a short time and also reproduces weed seeds very quickly. Each seed produces after its own kind.

> Be patient therefore, brethren, until
> the coming of the Lord. Behold the

farmer waits for the precious produce of the soil, being patient about it, until it gets the early and late rains. (James 5:7b, NASB)

Or I can plant an oak tree seed (acorn), and it will take years to produce a beautiful oak tree. When it produces, after its own kind, it is strong and mighty, and it will last for years or centuries. It will resist storms of rain and wind, resist disease from a destroyer becoming fruitful to produce quality products.

Scripture Assignment

Look up and write down promise scriptures that will hold you as you wait by faith. What are the promises in God's word can you think about?

Write down three *carrots* you are believing for:

1)
2)
3)

We are all called to produce seed and bear fruit and have authority in our lives. We have a right to take authority over the circumstances that directly affect us. Prayer is one of the tools and weapons given to us to help change our world.

> But when you ask, you must believe and not doubt, because the one who doubts is like a wave of the sea, blown and tossed by the wind. (James 1:6, NIV)

> Immediately the boy's father explained, 'I do believe; help me overcome my unbelief!' (Mark 9:24, NIV)

We are to increase in our faith. God does not fault us for being human in our faith but does want us to grow in believing and trusting Him.

> Then God said, "Let the earth sprout vegetation, plants yielding seed, and fruit trees bearing fruit after their kind, with seed in them, on the earth; and it was so. 12) And the earth brought forth vegetation, plants yielding seed after their kind, and trees bearing fruit, with seed in them, after their kind; and God saw that it was good. (Genesis 1:11–12, NASB)

When you are waiting for something to happen, what do you want to produce? You may need a car because you are on the bus or have to walk. You may have no choice than to purchase a car that is of little cost because you are not on a bus line or public transportation is not available at night when you need to get home from work. You may have children that you need to transport prior to work and need to drop them off safely. If you use the bus or walk, you may not get to your job on time. You may have to buy a low-cost car and would be thankful for a donated auto.

After receiving a low-cost vehicle that meets the immediate need, you don't have to give up your dream. You can still stand and believe for something better. With a low-cost vehicle, you may need to use your faith each month for repairs, extra oil, a new alternator, battery, tires, and starter, and it may not have air or heat in the vehicle. A low-cost auto may only get nine or ten miles of gas to the gallon. This is considered a "weed" that may be temporary (but necessary to cover the ground while you wait). Yes, it covers the ground if in the field and provides a temporary service to feed the birds, but a weed does not have a lot of value and does not provide a permanent support.

What are you willing to wait for?

Writer' Story

I pray it may encourage you in your waiting time.

I was without a vehicle after leaving domestic violence and needed to ride the bus. I could choose to get a cheap car that would get low gas mileage and may not be dependable or I could stay on the bus and believe for a better car. I was even doing job interview by bus. A misguided pastor blamed me for not having a car.

Still without a job, one day I won a one-year lease for a used vehicle. The company also provided the money for insurance, and the car was covered for repairs for the year. All I had to do was put gas in the car. At the end of the year, I was required to return the car; it had high miles of ninety-three thousand miles, and I was given the option to purchase the car. I appreciated the offer but also knew the vehicle had a problem with overheating. The blue book value was much lower than what the dealer wanted me to pay; the deposit they wanted was equal to the blue book value, and they wanted another eighteen months of very high payments. The car was not worth the asking price. At the end of the year, I returned the car and went back on the bus. Although tempted, I could not take the weed. I would wait for the "oak tree" car.

Seven months later, "I pulled a carrot" and received my good car, my acorn, oak-tree produced. I received a call from a financial institution that I could purchase a 2015 "current year-low mileage" vehicle at 4 percent interest. I was still doing job interviews, but the finance officer verified I could buy the car. Four years later, I still have the car, have never missed a payment, got excellent gas mileage, and added fifty thousand miles to the car.

What are you willing to stand and wait for? It may not be a car. It may be a house, better job, children, ministry. Are you willing to wait and stand? Can you wait? Is there a small weed you must put up with until you receive the bigger promise? Weeds grow overnight; an oak tree takes longer to produce but will stand through the big storms.

CHAPTER 5

I Have the Chewing Gum, Do You Have the Duct Tape? Let's Do This!

God's First Draft: Original

You pull up into a parking lot and notice a 1965 Chevrolet. It is the same year as the car you are driving, but it looks brand new. You examine the two 1965 Chevrolet automobiles and notice that the one you are sitting in and the one next to you are both are for sale. They are the same year, but the values are much different. The one you are driving you repaired yourself using items and tools from an old toolbox, the toolbox you found in a broken-down barn where you also discovered the abandoned '65 Chevy. Searching through the box, you found screwdrivers, duct tape, and an old pack of Wriggles chewing gum. You repaired the broken taillight with the duct tape and used the chewing gum to fasten the mirror to the dash.

Working under the hood, you got the car running. Using a screwdriver, you set the timing of the spark plugs. It sputters but now gets you back and forth to school and work. It only gets about seven miles to the gallon, leaks oil, and the seats have springs coming through. The passenger's floor has a big rust hole allowing mud and water to splash in the car when there is a storm. You can no longer tell what the original color of the car was, and the windshield is cracked. You were surprised when the car passed your state's vehicle inspection. You replaced the wipers, but they skip and drag on the window. When it is hot outside, you can't roll down the window because now you use a hanger to hold the window up. The heater to the car doesn't work, so it is better to keep the windows up when it's cold outside or snowing. You removed the hanger and left the windows down in summer only to find the floor of the car and seats soaking wet. The inside of the car was covered with ice stones from a hailstorm and hard rain. Now it has a smell of mold.

You have thought about letting the car go but must keep it for now. It is the only one you have. You're not sure if anyone sees enough value in it to pay for this broken-down car. You put effort into the repairs but still don't think it is worth much.

Your heart aches to now see the same year car next to the one you fixed. It is beautiful and worth so much more. You feel somewhat jealous.

The second 1965 Chevrolet vehicle is in original condition! Someone has taken the time to search for the original parts. The steering wheel and hubcaps look brand new. The leather and cloth seats were clean and have no tears. Someone has found the original seats from the manufacture and taken the time to meticulously stitch and install the cloth to the frame for the bucket seats.

Who would take such care and time to address every one of the small and large details? There are so many original details? The owner has also sanded the body of this other vehicle, carefully removing all rust, applying strong, rich metal to secure the original body of the car, making the paint smooth and glossy. There are no cracks in the frame or weakness that could be found. The car appears stronger than it was when it was originally designed.

The restorer has taken the time in removing all evidence of the old, faded, and cracked paint. After removing the rust and repairing the holes, new paint had been applied. But not just any paint color. The restorer searched and found the original paint color. The paint when applied would bring out the vibrate color and unique parts. This car is now restored to the original creation.

The owner walked up to the car and looks at you. "Do you want to hear how it runs?" he asks. "Let's go for a ride." You are scared but choose to trust him; he seems nice, and you want to see this uniquely restored car. You reluctantly get in on the passenger's side and put on your safety belt. The owner takes the car into neighborhoods with beautiful grass lawns and cool shaded streets.

The car runs with a quiet hum. The owner pulls into a gas station and fills the car with premium gas and a rich golden oil. He comes back to the car and hands you the keys. He tells you that even though this is a car made in the sixties, it gets thirty miles to the gallon. He tells you that he searched throughout the world to find all the original parts and paint. It has taken some time, but he wanted to do the job right and restore it to the original purpose and value. It wasn't time to give it to you until he knew you could trust him. He has been waiting for you to meet him at this time, and he is replacing the car that you repaired using your effort and limited resources. He says he has been watching you for a long time and has picked the perfect time. All the repairs, original parts, are totally paid for, and this gift is yours to keep.

He also tells you that he saw the pain that you were going through; he knew you were hurting. He watched as you tried to fix up the car you found abandoned in the barn. He was taking the time to restore this car and knew when you would be ready to give up the car you had been trying to keep fixed. Today you pulled into the parking lot. After you saw the other car, you knew that even though you tried to repair the rusted Chevy, it wasn't the best and took a lot of your money and time to keep it repaired and running. He is now telling you that the car, his original creation, he is giving to you, and he has been waiting for you to receive this beautiful car. Before today, you weren't fed up enough with the old car and not ready to let him give you the new. You are being restored to reach your original purpose.

Which vehicle is more valuable? They are the same year. What is difference in the value and why? One vehicle you restored with your limited tools with a found toolbox: chewing gum, duct tape, and screwdrivers. You did get the car running. The other vehicle was returned to its original condition. The restorer had richly used his resources and time to create value by first removing the old and bad that would create weakness in his chosen work. He then searched for the original parts, installing the parts with the right tools and picking the right paint. After the restorer had completed the search and remaking of the vehicle, he polished the work, creating a more valuable and stronger product. The 1965 vehicle could be used in its original purpose to reach new destinations. The restorer had made a thing of beauty for others to see.

Who is the vehicle that is being fixed? We are.

We can use our limited resources, time, and efforts to try to fix our own brokenness and receive some results. We may run around with broken lights, low tires, and slipping, coughing motors. We will not be able to reach our destination as efficiently, costing us more in gas, oil, repeated repairs, and time. We may or may not arrive to the destination; if we do arrive, we will come in late and distracted and noisy and no longer able to fulfill our ultimate purpose for being at the destination.

What if we allow the restorer to provide us the vehicle he wants for us? The restoration process may be painful as he sands and removes the rust. The removing of the rust may expose additional holes and even enlarge the holes to remove any damage around the holes. Before the restorer can apply the paint, he must search for and remove any additional cracks in our surface. He will be looking for blemishes and imperfections that may damage and scar the finished product of paint. He doesn't want his work to just look good on the outside, but he wants the work to be strong and withstand the pressures of the road.

He will also pay attention to the restoration and details of the inside. The seats need to be comfortable, for others sometimes may travel with us on our trips, and the dials of the dash need to be in the correct location for easy use.

God is a God of details. He will restore us to our original purpose. He also will, in the process, create a stronger and greater value by using what He originally created. He will take your history on the road, give it character and life, finding a purpose in His original destination for you. Your history is a part of your life journey. All the potholes in the road, curves, disasters, and detours, He will use as learning time between you and God. Let Him repair the road.

When driving your car, go forward. Occasionally there may be a glimpse in the rearview mirror. Take care of your new car. The danger is letting go of the wheel and climbing into the backseat to keep looking out the rear window.

Taking your focus off where you are going will lead to disaster and delays. Smile at your old self in the mirror. You now know the old is gone, and you are on a journey to explore new things and to see the beauty. Enjoy the trip. God has designed beauty and an exciting journey that will take you to the purpose He designed for you. On the trip, you may have some traveling companions for a while, supporters that may teach you knew things. With others, you may be able to mentor and have a conversation.

Leave behind the old road.

Remember the trip and your calling has no productive purpose to always repeat your negative story. We are not comparing bad stories. We do not want to use our story to bring attention to our self. Our story should be told sparingly and only when it magnifies and enhances the healing that God has done. Our story is a restoration story of God's goodness and glory. Never a victim story. Find the balance. Different audiences may hear different parts of your whole God story. Seek the Holy Spirit in, when, and how to share. God knows ahead of time who you will be sharing with and what they need to hear. He knows the part of your God story that will encourage the person in their own healing journey. It is the goodness of God not the weakness and tragedy that is our message.

God's first draft, the original: Repaired or restored. You need tools.

Assignment

In this exercise write out your victory God story. The restoration is still being done. Where do you see God's hand?

What are you able to tell people that will point them to God? Focus on the details of how God has been restoring you?

What is a short way you can speak about how you used to live in chaos? How can you expand how you now live in victory?

We are learning a new skill: To rethink how we view our world and life and learn to see our self as God see us. What does the good God, good Father think about us?

1) Replace negatives, being a victim or chaos views, with God's promises.

   Old mind thinking: Find scriptures that are opposite to the negative thoughts. Write down what God thinks about you and your success or value.
   Old Negative: I will always be this way because…
   God: Not true!
   Old Negative: I can't do it because…
   God: Not true.

Find other negative self-talk and beliefs you want to turn around. You are learning a new skill by learning the God truth about all of us. You are unique, and feel free to write down as many changes as you want. Turn negative beliefs to truth that God says about you.

2) Applying scripture and God's view: Where do you think you may someday use your gift and talents? How did your life journey affect the direction you are going? What positive strength did you learn that helps you now?

What negative history can you turn into a God story of victory that may now help others?

Have you discovered part of your God purpose? God created me to fulfill a purpose.

My purpose is to…

I can make a difference in…

CHAPTER 6

Broken Records: Letting Go of the Memories

In this chapter, you will look at how the negative words you have learned and now believe are stopping the vision of your God destiny. The negative words that you hear from yourself and others are lies from a broken and scratched vinyl record. Like vinyl records, your negative self-image is out of date. You are not the lies that you have heard.

> No weapon that is formed against you shall prosper; and every tongue that accuses you in judgment you will condemn. This is the heritage of the servants of the Lord, and their vindication is from Me, declares the Lord. (Isaiah 54:17, NASB)

God has created you for a different and successful life. In living, you are set on a path to discover that abundant life God wants to give you. It starts with a new recording that comes from God's studio.

> All things that the Father has are Mine, and I will disclose it to you. (John 16:15, NASB)

> For who among men knows the thoughts of a man except the spirit of the man, which is in him? Even so the thoughts of God no one knows except the Spirit of God. Now we have received, not the spirit of the world, but the Spirit who is from God, that we may know the things freely given to us by God, which things we also speak, not in words taught by human wisdom, but in those taught by the Spirit, combining spiritual thoughts with spiritual words. (1 Corinthians 2:11–13, NASB)

The old record.

Are you still listening to the old, negative records spinning in your thoughts? The one that is dull and irritating, drags and skips like an old warped record? Does it repeat, "You are stupid. You are stupid. You are nothing. They told and you are nothing, not worth anything. They were right. You knew they were right all the time. You are a failure. Hey, you will never get ahead."

> But I say, walk by the Spirit and you will not carry out the desires of the flesh. For the flesh sets its desires against the Spirit, and the Spirit against the flesh; for these are in opposition to one another, so that you may not do the things that you please. (Galatians 5:16–17, NASB)

What do we hear from the record today? Do you still hear that you are stupid or no good? Does the self-talk you say play like a scratched record? "You're stupid, you're stupid, you're stupid?" Or other negatives? How do you learn to play a new record? What do you tell yourself? Have you cut a new record with a new message creating a new soundtrack?

When you are hearing these negative lies, they are not coming from God. You do not have to listen to the liar anymore. You can learn how to shut down and not accept the lies. You can reject any words that is against the success God says you can have. Learn how to shatter the old record. A shattered record is impossible to hear.

> He was a murderer from the beginning, and does not stand in the truth, because there is no truth in him. Whenever he speaks a lie he speaks from his own nature; for he is a liar and the father of lies. (John 8:44b, NASB)

Broken Records: Letting Go of the Memories

Circle the phrases you say to yourself or have said to yourself. Write the date. These are the phrases you will be "shattering" and replacing with the truth that God's word says about you.

Still say   Used to say.

I'm too poor.
I have no education.
No one will give me a break.
I'm the wrong color.
I'm the wrong economic class.
I can't do it. It's too hard.
I belong in jail.
God will never forgive me.
God will not help me.
You may add other negatives you want to shatter when you become aware of them.
Other:
Other:

You Have a God Inheritance

Satan has always tried to take the inheritance of God's children, starting with Adam and Eve.

Jesus gave you back the right to your God inheritance. This is the new record that God created at the beginning of time. It has been waiting for you in His recording studio.

> The Spirit Himself bears witness with our spirit that we are children of God and if children, heirs also, heirs of God and fellow heirs with Christ, if indeed we suffer with Him in order that we may also be glorified with Him. (Romans 8:16–17, NASB)

God makes it clear that as you grow to know your heavenly father, you will hear the words of love from your heavenly father. You will learn more of the inheritance you already own. If someone does not know that a recording exists, and it is the recording of an inheritance, how can he make claim to what is in the will? If he finds out about the will but does not open it, how can he know all that he has been given? If there is property that is not claimed by the right heir, a false person can use false (counterfeit) documents and unlawfully claim the property and the inheritance. Producing false documents to stop your inheritance is what the devil has done. You have a right to take back the property and inheritance; God has already said it is yours.

What God says about you!

In the beginning, God created the heavens and the earth. In the beginning, God created His thoughts about you. He planned for you before the beginning of time. He made a purpose and time for you. You may have been born into an environment that told and showed you that you were not wanted. This is not what God thinks of you. You were wonderfully made with a purpose for a specific time and place. You have an assignment of greatness on your life. You are loved, treasured, and the apple of God's eye.

> For thou didst form my inward parts; thou didst weave me in my mother's womb. I will give thanks to Thee, for I am fearfully and wonderfully made; Wonderful are Thy works, and my soul knows it very well. (Psalm 139:13–16, NASB)

> For I am confident of this very thing, that He who began a good work in you will perfect it until the day of Christ Jesus. (Philippians 1:6, NASB)

You are not an abandoned child. You are not junk because God does not make mistakes. In His plan, you are made as excellent. Your body is not perfect. You may even have a disability that you deal with every day, but God sees you as perfect—a design He created. You are a success, you have great value, you are wonderfully made. God created you in His image.

> For you did not receive a spirit that makes you a slave again to fear, but you received the Spirit of sonship (adoption). And by him we cry, "Abba, Father." (Romans 8:15, NIV)

Your history did not stop your assigned purpose. In all your mistakes, in all the harshness that you have lived through, you still have a divine purpose. You have not blown the plan. You did not mess up so much that God cannot get you back on track. God's bigger and wiser than all your messed-up choices and will bring you back to center. You gave up. He did not. You quit. He did not. You believed you were damaged. He sees the value in you. You are wonderfully made, a jewel, a present to be given and cherished. How do you know?

> Because he has loved Me, therefore I will deliver him; I will set him securely on high because he has known My name, He will call upon Me, and I will answer him; I will be with him in trouble; and rescue him, and honor him. (Psalm 91:14–15, NASB)

He is our savior and a just and true God. He can turn things around. God is a healer of emotional and physical hurts. God can restore you to your original purpose and transform your circumstances to the perfect plan. God gives life in excellence and doesn't repair like an old car but restores to the original priceless plan He created for you.

Everyone's purpose is to help others. You will find some of the answers will come from your past. No matter how ugly your experiences have been, the past is a key to your purpose. Where you were hurt the most is where you can gain insight about your strengths and talents. God will teach you how to use your history and how to apply the skills and talents you have been given.

He saw you. He trained you, and He protected you. You are still alive when others wanted to kill you. When you thought of suicide, when you were in the wrong place, when you made wrong choices, God still and will always love you.

Your still alive to make right choices to learn from where you came from to let God heal and transform you into your purpose. Now you are to move forward; don't give up.

> For you have made the Lord, my refuge, even the Most High, your dwelling place. No evil will befall you, Nor will any plague come near your tent. For He will give His angels charge concerning you, to guard you in all your ways. (Psalm 91:9–11, NASB)

Create a new record, break the old one. Don't just break it; shatter it. When you find the old record in the recess of your mind (like finding a record in the secondhand store), remember you don't want the seconds anymore; you want something new. You want to start playing God's new life-giving recording—the one that says you are a gift to the world, your family, and your community. You have a definite purpose and you have value.

The toughest person to convince will be yourself. You are with you all the time and have been listening to the broken record of negatives for too many years. You are the one who can talk yourself down and convince yourself you are not good enough and that you don't deserve to be happy. You're the one who puts up roadblocks, stalls, and cheats yourself. It is time to stop telling yourself the loudest and biggest lies of how bad you think you are!

How do you renew your thinking?

When you have been weak, God is strong. When you did not think God was there, He was. When you blame Him for what happened to you, He never meant the bad to happen. Humanity entered and caused pain. It was never God's plan for you to be hurt. He did not turn His back. He saw the hurt you went through. He wanted to stop the pain, to take you out of the chaos. He left you here to live. God allowed man to choose, and evil entered in.

If you are trying to do self-talk the way the world may say to do self-talk, you are going down the wrong road. New age is not the answer. The road you want to take is the God road. There will always be counterfeits to the plan God first made.

There are excellent speakers and programs in the world. Listening to and hearing these speakers may help you develop new habits and gain tools and ideas. You will know when God is speaking and when the information just doesn't feel comfortable. All information that is based on God's word principles can be brought back to God's word. An example is that today there are people who give into needs of the world populations. You will see that they are oftentimes very blessed and continue to grow in abundance. They may or may not be a believer in God's word. The principle of sowing and reaping is still active. God's blessing is still active and evident in their life. If those who may not believe in God's promises and word are able to bless others, then as believers, we can be a greater blessing to the world and spread the word of salvation. Start where you are in your giving. Let God teach you. There are plenty of opportunities to give into good ministries and God's work. God will direct you where you are to give. When you do not give to one ministry but feel led to give to another, do the giving to where God leads you.

We all obey the laws of God's creation. Gravity works in the world for the believer and unbeliever alike.

Protect Your New Recording

Not everyone should be heard. You are starting to hear and believe the new record. Letting go of the old vinyl record may be hard to release, but it is not an antique. It is scratched and has no value.

There are records to discard as you are developing your new recordings.

> And these are the ones by the wayside where the word is sown. When they hear, Satan comes immediately and takes away the word that was sown in their heart. (Mark 4:15, NKJV)

Listening to gossip and drama of family and neighbors does not lift you up. It is part of the old record and may be a habit to break. You may want to be polite. Standing firm to limit what you are listening to may come off to the intruder as rude. Working on your new blessed life will come with resistance from others who are not working on goals. It is important to take care of yourself. When someone brings gossip to your door, they are not polite. Telling you gossip is not respecting your time, and they are most likely saying negatives about you to others. Politely tell the person you don't want to hear what they are saying. You may need to repeat yourself on several occasions. "I don't want to hear it. What you are saying is none of my business."

They may say, "I just thought you should know."

No, you should not know. God gives us authority. Our authority does not extend into everyone else's life. Recognize when you have authority to help, when you should help (not always), and when others should help themselves. Helping those who are always needy becomes a drain of your time and energy. Allow God to be their source and other community resources. The trailblazers of the neighborhood will soon get the message that you are not going to listen and you are not going to solve problems that do not belong to you.

Everyone has a goal even if they do not say they do. The gossip or negative speaker and constant complainer is the person who has made their daily goal to stir up drama in the neighborhood. Most of the time, they are after attention and enjoy creating drama and chaos.

You are on the road to a better life. Not everyone is going to support you.

What is the truth? How much and how long are you going to listen to others? How powerful are they in your self-talk voice that you hear? How do you break the cycle? Start with you. If you have been listening to others who say how negative you are, you started to believe what they said. Your self-worth is tattooed and programed from the beginning with negatives. It is not going to be easy to change or erase the tattoos. Every day learn and apply scriptures of God's promises. God says you are wonderfully made, and His voice is the one you want to recognize. By rereading (if you can out loud) His plan for you, your inner spirit man begins to replace the old lies with the truth. You start to believe what you listen to.

God's truth says you are valuable and have a purpose. You may not even know your purpose yet. It is to help others, and you will find that some of the answers will come from your past. No matter how ugly your experiences have been, the past is a key to your purpose. Where you were hurt the most is where you can gain insight and learn to apply your gifts and talents to help the most.

God does love you. He never forgot you. He has His thoughts on you every day. He wants to show you how He loves you. The past is over. Let Him step in and heal your hurt. What happened to you was not His choice for you. It is a choice to let Him into the healing process. The new recording will be beautiful.

What does God think of you? You are a jewel, you have a purpose, you are the apple of His eye, you have a divine destiny. That you are already a success, you have value, you are wonderfully made. God created you in His image. He is your savior and a just and true God. He can turn things around. God will make things right. God is a healer of emotional and physical hurts. God can restore you to your original purpose and transform your circumstances to the perfect plan. God gives life in excellence and doesn't repair like an old, dried-up tape recording. He restores to the original priceless plan He created for you.

> I glorified thee on the earth having accomplished the work which thou hast given me to do. And now glorify thou me together with thyself father with the glory which I had with thee before the world was. (John 17:4–5, NASB)

> And this I pray that your love may abound still more and more in real knowledge and all discernment so that you may approve the things that are excellent in order to be sincere and blameless until the day of Christ. (Philippians 1:9–10, NASB)

> Now I want you to know brothers that my circumstances have turned out for the greater progress of the gospel so that my imprisonment in the cause of Christ has become well know through the whole praetorian guard and to everyone else and that most of the rather trusting in the Lord because of my imprisonment have far more courage to speak the word of God without fear. (Philippians 1:12–14, NASB)

We are created out of our circumstances. You make a choice to be strong. What you went through is what will be able to help others. Others will look at your life as a testimony of God's and your success. Believing lies and living in self-pity is one choice. Your second choice is to change your mind-set and follow the destiny God made. In doing so, you become the beautiful person that God our creator already sees you as. He sees the finished product. He does not hear the broken record playing over your life. He hears the promises that He has made to you. God cannot lie. He made you promises, and He must keep those promises to you. He sees you through His creative eye. He calls you to your purpose out of the muck and mud. You are a "pressed down, shaken together, running over" promise of fulfillment on His team, a child of God, prince or princess, who is to overcome the principals of evil. The past destruction plan of the devil is void. Overcome the negative. Move into the future, and live a successful, purposeful life that God crated you to live. King's kids have the best of life—abundance of food, care, watchful eyes to protect them and joy.

Challenge yourself today to reach the promise God has set before you. Who are you in Him? See yourself not as the broken, hurt, damaged, and scared little person. See yourself as the beautiful child God made. You belong to a loving Father—the chosen child who lives a life of play, joy, secure and protected by your heavenly Father. If you did not have a good role model for a father, ask yourself how God would have treated you in that situation. God can become the good Father you never had. How can He help you now? How powerful is God? He is not weak. You cannot put Him into a box. He created the stars. He created you. You are not junk; you are the only you. Even if you are an identical twin, there is still just one you. Challenge yourself to see you the way God sees you—beautiful, strong, wise, perfect, on a direction that may have been off course for a while but has a divine destiny and purpose. When you reach your God-given abundant life, you will help others. Others need to learn how to live in abundant freedom. As a life model, you can teach others what God's success looks like: wholeness of mind, spirit, physically well, chemically sound, growing wiser, learning to cope, learning new love and skills, teaching others, strengthened in the inner man, seeking and growing in challenges.

It is not easy to walk the way we are to walk. There is a challenge to find our purpose. Even when you know the basic of your purpose and maybe the "title" of the role you are to be, you need direction. What is the definition or the direction of that role? How do you apply the God principles to the destiny you have been given? How do you walk in victory and how do you reach others with the strength of God? Who has God placed into your path to mentor? Who is in your path just for a fleeting moment? Who will be affected by you when you speak a single and word send a smile and never see again? Who are you to meet to encourage today?

Who do you show grace to?

Others are responsible for their life choices. You or I can't fix it for them. We can be a role model. Demonstrate the love of God and promises of God. At some point, they will need to grow into the promises that God made for them. You cannot reach your purpose in God carrying someone on your back. For a short period, you may carry them, show them by example, and give them tools of information and God's word promises. Let them know what they can have. Watch for and use wisdom when letting a person be responsible for their outcome. You are not a failure if they fall. You also cannot take credit for their success. They have a choice with information they receive from you or from others. They will need to process the information and learn to correctly apply the information they receive. If they ignore what God has told them, it is their choice.

If someone comes back for more tools, be willing to give them a new tool. Are they being a good steward with the information they receive? Have the applied the last God wisdom they were given? If their need is above your skill level, don't be afraid to make a referral to a better fit for the need. Be willing to let them go. Let them find the person or information that will be able to teach them, bring them more healing, and guide them. You cannot be someone else's only source or their god. You may have been put in their life for a short time. God is a good God; we are all created as individuals with unique talents. Only God can lead us to the one who can relate to us the best. Someone who is struggling may be helped by a trusted minister, counselor, or youth director. Healing can come from hearing the instruction of the Lord from a good sermon preached under the influence of the Holy Spirit.

Create New Records: Letting Go of the Memories

Create a new record, break the old one. Don't just break; it shatter it! When you find the old record in the recess of your mind (like finding a record in the secondhand store), remember you don't want the seconds anymore; you want something new to put on a new life-giving recording, the one that says you are a gift to the world, your family, your friends, you have a purpose, and you have value.

Stay alert to catch old habits and negatives that want to derail God's word.

God has planted within you unique gifts and talents. It is your job to discover what He has already put in you. As you get to know more about God's promises, character, and love, you will grow closer to your assignment by reading His word, learning to talk Him and listen for His directions, and spending time in prayer and worship. Seek after Him; get to know Him.

You are created, and now your circumstances are a part of your uniqueness. Someday make the choice to be stronger because of what you experience.

You are stronger in your faith. Learn how to pray for others. Allow the wayward adult child, sister, brother, family member, acquaintance to come back to God through your prayers. Know that God can bring a God-fearing person that will lead the family member back to Him. Pray for an open heart, open eyes, open spirit, and the seeds will keep growing.

Scripture is not the only way to break the negative records. There is an anointed worship and Christian music available in the United States and other countries. Make use of these resources when they are available. Music and worship can bring healing and penetrates the soul and spirit.

Most music is replaced with new sound. Even worship music is evolving. Old sounds still move us, and new sounds take us deeper. We are to always grow and discover new facets of God's love.

Scriptures from God's Word to Start Writing Your New Record

This is not an exhaustive list. Take time to discover many other promise scriptures that you can apply to your life.

> This book of the law shall not depart from your mouth but you shall meditate on it day and night, so that you may be careful to do according to all that is written in it; for then you will make your way prosperous, and then you will have success. (Joshua 1:8, NASB)

> So, faith comes from hearing and hearing by the word of Christ. (Romans 10:17, NASB)

> Pleasant words are a honeycomb, Sweet to the soul and healing to the bones. (Proverbs 16:24, NIV)

> And do not be conformed to this world, but be transformed by the renewing of your mind, that you may prove what the will of God is, that which

is good and acceptable and perfect. (Romans 12:2, NASB)

Behold, I will bring to it health and healing, and I will heal them; and I will reveal to them an abundance of peace and truth. (Jeremiah 33:6, NASB)

Call to Me, and I will answer you, and I will tell you great and mighty things, which you do not know. (Jeremiah 33:3, NASB)

Guard the good deposit that was entrusted to you—guard it with the help of the Holy Spirit who lives in us. (2 Timothy 1:14, NASB)

Blessing scriptures: Philippians 4:19, 2 Corinthians 9:8, Psalm 23:1, Deuteronomy 8:18, Matthew 6:33, Ephesians 3:20, Luke 6:38,

Seeking direction scriptures: Isaiah 48:17b (NIV), "I am the Lord your God who teaches you to profit, who leads you in the way you should go," and Book of Proverbs

Healing scriptures: Jeremiah 17:14, Psalm 107:20, Psalm 103:2–5, 1 Peter 2:24, Romans 8:11, Psalm 118:17, Isaiah 53:5, Malachi 4:2

Faith scriptures: Mark 11:22–23, 2 Corinthians 1:20, Philippians 2:13, Hebrews 11, 1 John 5:14–15, Hebrews 10:23, John 14:1, Matthew 18:19–20,

Peace scriptures: 2 Corinthians 1:2–4, Psalm 43:5, 2 Timothy 1:7, Romans 12:2, Proverbs 23:7

CHAPTER 7

Who Told You that You Are Stupid?

We are all born into this world and eventually want to know our purpose. No directions for your outcome was written on your forehead. You start off as a vulnerable and innocent person. Some entered into homes of love from healthy relationships, a parent, mother and father, or safe relative. You may receive encouragement from another person who entered your life: teacher, foster parent, mentor, grandparent, or trusted neighbor.

Everyone learns the rules of life and love from the world around them.

You may have been taught a different reality, an opposite life of rejection that created your reality of being unwanted, unloved, or discarded. You may have learned from someone who caused fear, took advantage, abused, beat you down emotionally, physically. You may have heard only negatives; you are worthless, stupid, no good, and dirty. This may have been the only attention (even though negative) you received; the one who violated your trust caused confusion, and you learned from the negative words and behavior of others that you are unloved by the world.

Today you may believe and still hear some of the lies of the enemy: "you are no good," "not wanted," "just like your father or mother, and they are no good," "you are stupid," "can't do anything right," "why can't you be like…," "you'll never amount to anything," "you were never wanted," "you are too poor, have no educated, in the wrong economic class, have wrong skin color or not a good enough Christian." All these negatives are lies.

> He was a murderer from the beginning, and does not stand in the truth, because there is no truth in him. Whenever he speaks a lie, he speaks from his own nature; for his is a liar and the father of lies. (John 8:44b, NASB)

God can enter your life, and He tells you the truth. God wants to bring you the right kind of love. God does want to heal your pain and teach you the image and value He knows is in you.

> In the same way God desiring even more to show to the heirs of the promise the unchangeableness of His purpose, interposed with an oath, in order that by tow unchangeable things, in which 'it is impossible for God to lie', we may have strong encouragement, we who have fled for refuge in laying hold of the hop set before us. (Hebrews 6:17–18, NASB)

Stop: Take time to pray about the hurt and negatives you have been told to believe. Ask God to come into the pain and start the healing. You are going to reach into God's word and replace the enemy's lies and replace the negative with the truth promises of God. God has always loved you and desires to enter your life and show you His unfailing pure love, a love that is healthy without lies.

What does God say? Who are you? God's first draft original.

What does the Bible say about you? What is the truth about God's love for you?

God says you are an original, designed for the time you were born. Even if you are an identical twin, you are still an original. You have personality traits unique to you and thoughts and ideas that are only your own. You own every thought and idea within you. You may tell yourself negative or positive thoughts. All thoughts create your belief about the world around you and also creates your future.

God saw you. He trained you, and He protected you. You are still alive when others wanted to kill you. When you thought of suicide, when you were in the wrong place, when you made wrong choices, God still loves you. You are here to make right choices and learn from your past. Your past will not make you since until you allow God to create something beautiful. Now you are to move forward; you are being transformed into your divine purpose. Some of the process of erasing the negatives in history may hurt. Don't give up! You want your better life.

> For I am confident of this very thing, that He who began a good work in you will perfect it until the day of Christ Jesus. (Philippians 1:6, NASB)

In Paul's life, he suffered multiple beatings, was imprisoned, and faced death. He writes in Philippians chapter 1 of the suffering he went through. He recognized the positive impact on the guards and prisoners, and his suffering had been an encouragement to all the body of Christ. He received word that others were showing courage while being persecuted for taking a stand in God. He found a purpose in the suffering. God can show you how the pain you experienced, you can learn from and develop a skill that will encourage others.

Paul had a purpose and was told of the suffering ahead of time. Paul had killed many believers prior to his own believing. He would now suffer to take the word of God to the world.

> But the Lord said to him, "Go, for his is a chosen instrument of Mine, to bear My name before the Gentiles and kings and the sons of Israel; for I will show him how much he must suffer for My name's sake." (Acts 9:15–16, NASB)

You don't have to tell your detailed story (you are no longer a victim). You are a product of your learning, and now it's a part of your God purpose. Paul's testimony helped others fulfill the call. Your learning road can help others recognize the goodness of God and discover that they also have a God purpose. Always point to God, the ultimate wisdom and healer.

You are not junk because God does not make junk. You are made with His excellence in mind. Your body is not perfect. You may even have a disability that you deal with every day, but God sees you as perfect, a design He created with a history that leads to your assigned purpose. In all your mistakes, in all the harshness that you have lived through, you still have a divine purpose. You have not blown the plan. You did not mess up so much that God cannot get you back on track. God's bigger and wiser than all your messed-up choices and will bring you back to center. You gave up. He did not. You quit. He did not. You believed you were damaged. He sees the beautiful value in you. You are wonderfully made, a jewel, a present to be given and cherished. God says this truth about you:

> Thy hands made me and fashioned me; Give me understanding that I may learn Thy commandments. (Psalm 119:73, NASB)

> For you created my inmost being, you knit me together in my mother's womb. (Psalm 139: 13, NIV)

> Before I formed you in the womb, I knew you, before you were born, I set you apart. (Jeremiah 1:5a, NIV)

> You gave me life and showed me kindness, and your providence watched over my spirit. (Job 10:12, NIV)

> For I know the plans I have for you; declares the Lord, plans to prosper you and not to harm you, plans to give you hope and a future. (Jeremiah 29:11, NIV)

> For I know the plans that I have for you, declares the Lord, plans for welfare and not for calamity, to give you a future and a hope. (Jeremiah 29:11, NASB)

> Again, the kingdom of heaven is like a merchant looking for fine pearls. When he found one of great value he went away and sold everything he had and bought it. (Matthew 13:45–46, NIV)

God created something and everything out of nothing. He spoke, and His words came forth with energy creating everything into time. His creative power is still extending the universe. New stars are being formed. Planets are starting to turn. Gases and explosions are going on in space and the universe. He created by a single word "*let*" into space. That "*let*" is still producing today. Millions of light-years, by our measurement, creation is still producing a perfect plan.

How long did God take to make His plan for the universe and us? Less than a micro, microsecond. That plan is still producing. *Let* is a solid word, a single command. No, let's think about it first; maybe we will, but let it become. God created with a word of His will. In His original speaking to make creation, He also created the plan and time for you to be born and fulfill your purpose.

You have a choice to make to fulfill your purpose.

Jesus had to make a decision to line up with the will of God. He was sent to earth to complete a purpose. Jesus was aware that He would be experiencing great pain. He asked His Father God if there was any other way to save the world.

In Matthew 26, Jesus said. "Not my will but thine be done." Jesus lined up with the will of the God.

> And He took with Him Peter and the two sons of Zebedee, and began to be grieved and distressed. Then He said to them, "My soul is deeply grieved, to the point of death; remain here and keep watch with Me." And He went a little beyond them, and fell on His face and prayed, saying, "My Father if it is possible, let this cup pass from Me; but not as I will but as Thou will." (Matthew 26:37–39, NASB)

Jesus knew of the God plan before He came to be born. He still did not want to suffer unless it was the only way to save the people God had created. God desires fellowship with us. In John 1:1, we learn that Jesus was at creation and was the word:

> In the beginning was the word and the word was with God and the word was God. He was in the beginning with God. All things came into being by Him, and apart from Him nothing came into being that has come into being. In Him was life, and the life was the light of men. And the light shines in the darkness and the darkness did not comprehend it. (NASB)

Jesus was part of the beginning, the Spirit hovered over the vastness, and God spoke the word *let*: Jesus was the light that was spoken into the answer. He was a part of the original thought plan.

Light is energy. Light is moving. Short and long waves create colors that you see. Sound is moving waves of energy. In space, creation continues growing and creating new sound, vibrant lights, and energy. Space is not dark. You cannot see the beauty of the galaxy of gases, stars, and movement without the help of magnification. It takes faith to believe in the beauty, movement, and continued creation of space. You cannot see the activity from earth. The creation is not dark where stars and galaxies are forming and collapsing.

Outer space also has a pulse. Just like the most inner part of your smallest body cell within the nucleus is a pulse, set like a pendulum keeping time, also outer space is pulsing, keeping time. In God's creation, from greatest to smallest, is the sound of God's heartbeat.

> For you will go out with joy, and be led forth with peace; The mountains and the hills will break forth into shouts of joy before you, and all the trees of the field will clap their hands. (Isaiah 55:12, NASB)

Mighty is our God that could make such a perfect plan that everything in His plan would carry a time clock and energy. From the smallest unseen in our body, the table that looks solid to the vast outer space that rotates, pulses with time. Still expanding with the beginning of *let* spoken into, creating energy from nothing. Out of nothing. Came everything.

> And saying, "Where is the promise of His coming? For ever since the fathers fell asleep, all continues just as it was

from the beginning of creation." (2 Peter 3:4, NASB)

You also have power in your words. You create by speaking. Your words come from your beliefs. It does not matter if your words are correct or negative. Your negative words create and contribute to your negative outcomes. Your positive words create faith within you and the belief that there is a better way to live. Adding and learning of God's promises and word about who He says you are and what you are to Him is important. His word will help you to replace any negative beliefs that you have been wrongly taught. As His child, you are given and can receive all the good He wants you to have.

> Therefore, everyone who hears these words of Mine, and acts upon them, may be compared to a wise man who built his house upon the rock. (Matthew 7:24, NASB)

> So, faith comes by hearing and hearing by the word of Christ. (Romans 10:17, NASB)

> For the word of God is living and active and sharper than a two-edged sword, and piercing as far as the division of soul and spirit, of both joints and marrow, and able to judge the thoughts and intentions of the heart. (Hebrews 4:12, NASB)

> For by these He has granted to us His precious and magnificent promises, in order that by them you might become partakers of the divine nature, having escaped the corruption that is in the world by lust. (2 Peter 1:4, NASB)

If you were born into chaos, you still can learn to identify with the plan that God made for you. He created you in the original plan, and the design included that you would be born at a certain time. He created a unique plan and purpose for you. You have a destiny. Your job is to discover that plan and fulfill the plan. You may have grown up in pain. You may have had a happy childhood but later in life experienced pain, but *you choose your future.*

Because of the pain, you renew vivid memories that now control your life, sabotaging your potential for a good future with destructive behavior. You may hurt so deeply that others have become victims of your anger, sometimes you may hurt them in the same way that you were hurt.

Yes, God loves you. Remember He had a perfect plan for creation. Part of that perfect plan was the creation of man. In creating humans, He created a free-thinking, creative being. If there were no thought process created in man, God could have…with the angels.

Part of creation and God making humans in His image was also giving man a creative part that could think, analyze, and come to a personal conclusion of choice to love God.

Along with this creative part, man has created negative and harmful thoughts, created thoughts that harm others and himself. This is the destructive part of man. We are not perfect. We are created in God's image and have the right to a free choice.

The harmful abuse you experienced did not come from God but from the wrongful thoughts and creation of the one(s) who hurt you. The person who hurt you may have been yourself. Could not have God changed His plan and put you into a better environment? Didn't He see that you would be hurt?

You were in the beginning thoughts of God in the beginning of creation (scripture). It was not His plan that changed; it was man's. God is all-knowing, and He sees the beginning to the end. He knew that by the time you came to be born on the earth. He designed a perfect plan for you to seek Him. He also designed a way out of your pain.

So, did God mean for you to be hurt? Can you blame God? Why didn't God stop the chaos if He loves you? If God was love, He must love you. When you doubt His love, He still set a plan to get you out of the chaos. God loves you like a *good* farther loves His child. You are not a mistake. You are worth being loved.

God is love. He did not want me to be born into chaos. He did not plan in the beginning. Humans choose to sin, to hurt. You are not responsible for where you were born. You are not responsible for the bad choices others made. You can choose to remove yourself from a toxic situation even if it is a parent. Yes, you honor you father and mother knowing that they gave you life. You have now come to know that God is your good parent.

Through God's patience and teaching, you can learn that He loves you enough to take the negative and turn it into something of healing. And through that as you learn to be healed, you can now bring healing to others.

If you have heard and believed the negatives all your life, it may take time to believe that God does love you.

Know what God says about you is more powerful than the negative that you tell yourself. Take the old record, and break it. It will no longer play the negative words in your head. Old vinyl records are hard to break, and the messages in your head that you have heard for years are hard to overcome.

Let God help you get over the negative. You are not doing it on someone else's time. God does not want you to continue to live in the negative image and pain anymore. Only with God can you come out of the pain. Only with God can you start to see yourself the way He created you. Only with God can you see yourself as one who can be loved. Only with God can you start to feel safe and secure. Only with God can you come into the plan He created you to be. The first step is to learn who you are arranged for this time and according to His image. The first step is knowing He does love you. You may not believe it yet, but He does. He does not make mistakes.

Yes, He could have placed you with a different family. You were born into the situation that you were born into. You came into the situation that hurt you. Your tragedy that happened is not the final outcome. It did not destroy you even though you thought it did. It did not destroy you even though you think it still will. You made it. You are getting stronger. You are in a process of living out the Bible. You are an overcomer. You have a right to take back all that Satan stole from you. You will not do the conquering in a negative way with a God plan. Seek God's original plan for you and move in the same direction of His plan. Recognize the value that He created in you.

> I am my beloved's and His desire is for me. (Song of Solomon 7:10, NASB)

No matter how much you desire God, His desire and longing for a personal relationship with you is even greater than you can imagine.

God will someday bring you to a point that you may help others out of their pain.

You will be able to show others through God's plan that they are loved. They have a purpose, and God can bring them into a place that is designed for them. Their life plan is not the same as your life plan. You will travel and meet people whom they will not meet. They will become whole in God and be able to then speak healing and wisdom into others.

Don't let anyone tell you "just get over it." Do make a choice to let God heal you. Let the healing begin today. Let Him purge the pain as deep and as fast as He knows you can stand. Don't choose to stay in the pain. Realize it may have become a part of your DNA. Allow God to change the DNA image you have of being in pain and the idea it will always be a part of your life. If the pain has become your best friend, choose this day if you want to live a life like this, the old way, or you want to live the life God promised you. It is a choice.

You do deserve to have a quality, productive life; you are not stupid, a looser. You can have the plan that God has purposed for you. You may have gotten off track from the plan you may have been born into, which is in chaos. But God can restore you to an original plan. The first step is to allow Him to enter, meet you just where you're at, accept you with all your mistakes, clean you up, straighten up your thoughts, and heal you emotionally. It is a choice. Start to climb that mountain. No one can do it for you. You may need to leave some people behind. Because you will start to leave the negative history behind.

Assignment

Make an active choice to make a change to a better, good future. The first step may be to accept Jesus Christ as your savior. Becoming a child of God, you will have all the inherence and promises of the child of a king.

The second step is to recognize and start to believe that God of all creation is a loving God.

Review the scriptures from the last two chapters. Write down scriptures of how God see you as valuable. Use your Bible reference materials to discover and write down other promises that God has given. What promises can you share in the group or find that you can take hold of and believe?

CHAPTER 8

In the Deep River? Turn Around and Float Downstream for a While!

Before the first rain was seen on the earth, God provided the materials for Noah's ark. He selected Noah, a man of great faith who believed the words of God the creator. A flood would come and cover the earth. Noah was obedient to follow every detailed instruction from God. Within these instructions were God's plan to save Noah's family and the repopulate of earth.

If Noah had refused to listen, he would not have been able to navigate and survive the problems of the flood. The instructions also provided a supply of animals. Noah would use some of these animals for sacrificial offering of praise and thanksgiving. Noah listened in faith, took action, and survived the future chaos. He thanked and praised God for wisdom, provision, and protection.

You may have experienced a great flood in your life. This may not have been a natural flood but a flood of crisis in your family, health, finances, trauma, loss, legal, or emotional. In your flood of life, the water was deep, dark, and unpredictable. It was destructive and caught you by surprise. In this chapter, you will look at one way of viewing a major problem. You will also look at a way of handling the problem. There are more ways to handle problems that are not listed in this chapter. God can give you creative ways and spiritual insight to answers.

Everyone experiences problems. Some problems may seem overwhelming. You feel like you are in very deep water and trapped. You look for a solution and see no way out. The deep river will not let up and is pounding you in the back as it relentlessly keeps coming. The river and flooding seem overwhelming.

The flood of water (your crisis) came from upstream and continued to build until it surprised you. You could not foresee the problem or may have seen a far-off storm cloud. The flood is now here, causing destruction; you are losing your footing. You desperately need a way to survive.

Time may become your only survival tool.

There may be times when all you can do is turn around and face the water. In doing so, you can see some dangers and details of the problems headed your way. Your only choice may be to take a deep breath, lean back (into the problem), and float down the river for a while. You make a decision to commit to the journey. Your only immediate resource is time for problem solving. You pray that soon you will be able to travel downstream and touch ground again.

You are not in control of the wild journey. At first, you are unable to relax. You noticed that you are not alone. The weight of your body is supported. The direction you are being taken seems planned. You just missed a large boulder and travelled through the intense rapids in safety. Are there still rapids ahead? God carried you through the danger, the waterfall, and over a major part of the chaos. Can you look back and recognize when God carried you safely over the waterfall? How did you feel? Scared and afraid?

You are still getting wet, but now notice the river is becoming calmer. Take another deep breath, and relax.

You are still surrounded by the problem, caught in the journey down the river. Close your eyes for a while. God's hand is holding you throughout the entire journey. With this support, you begin to feel more water that supports your body. Is it warm, cold, cool to the touch? You feel the gentle bounce of the current. God is carrying you fast sometimes and then slow. You start to notice a change in the journey. The river is wider and less intense. Is it time for you to stand up yet? You look for a safe exit to shore. Your exit must be on calm and secure ground.

God allows us to go through life journeys even if we would like to be rescued. There are reasons for the journey down river.

Things we can learn from a journey down the river (journey through an overwhelming problem):

1) You may learn to trust God and others.

What will you face when you get out of the water? Are you comfortable and safe in the water flow and cradled in the arms of God? What are you learning? The provisions, the safety in danger, and rough current, the calmness of His Spirit? Do you see bridges, train tracks, evidence of people on the move? Where are you in God's plan?

> Be anxious for nothing, but in everything by prayer and supplication

> with thanksgiving let your request be made know to God. (Philippians 4:6, NASB)

> In the day of prosperity be happy, but in the day of adversity consider— God has made the one as well as the other so that man may not discover anything that will be after him. (Ecclesiastes 7:14, NASB)

2) Be thankful. Within the worse problems, we can still find beauty around us.

Look for and recognize some beauty as you are carried through your problem. What colors can you see? Close your eyes, and open them to see something new, like shade trees at the riverbank. Know that you may catch of glimpse of God watching you as sun was peeping through the large trees. The oaks have large arms that give you shade as they covered and protected you from the heat. You notice birds with songs and nest, new life and spiders busy creating webs. All because of God's design. Did you see animals who came to drink from the river?

> Finally, brethren, whatever is true, whatever is honorable, whatever is right, whatever is pure, whatever is lovely, if there is any excellence and if anything, worthy of praise let your mind dwell on these things. (Philippians 4:8, NASB)

3) Forgiveness. You may have taken part in the problem.

Even if you helped cause the problem, you may have learned not to make the same choice next time or take the same action. Your lesson may be a new strength to say no to a temptation.

    a) Ask God for forgiveness. He does forgive. Receive God's forgiveness, then forgiven yourself.

And the prayer offered in faith will restore the one who is sick, and the Lord will raise him up, and if he has committed sins, they will be forgiven him. (James 5:15, NASB)

    b) Forgive anyone who hurt you. As a victim of a wrong, still forgive.

Let all bitterness and wrath and anger and clamor and slander be put away from you, along with all malice. And be kind to one another, tender-hearted, forgiving each other, just as God in Christ also has forgiven you. (Ephesians 4:31–32, NASB)

4) Forgive and make a better plan.

On your river trip, you may have learned how you are contributing to your own hurt. There are unbalanced relationships.

Set limits, and make a plan to reach your God purpose goals. You are delaying or can totally derail your future when you allow yourself to "use others as an accuse." The things you spend your time on today will create your tomorrow. Change comes in the small steps from one stone river to the next. A person who doesn't belong in your plan is like a stone with moss. They will cause you to lose balance and slip into the river.

You are now more aware when someone wants to use you to meet their needs. Respect your resources and time by learning to say *no*. Are you guilty of enabling others to be dependent on you? If so, what are you getting out of their neediness for you? Do you complain later that they use you and your time even when you have not taken responsibility to set firm and clear *no* boundaries. You can choose how to get to the shore. Some distractions will take you in the wrong direction.

5) You can now give back and teach others.

Can you now meet someone else's need? Metaphorically, did you see a broken fence, an animal that got loose, a dry crop that needed rain? Did you see abuse of the land or abuse of a person that you may someday be able to help?

> And be kind to one another, tender-hearted, forgiving each other, just as God in Christ also has forgiven you. (Ephesians 4:32, NASB)

> The fear if the Lord us the beginning of knowledge; Fools despise wisdom and instruction. (Proverbs 1:7, NASB)

> For let not that man expect that he will receive anything from the Lord, being a double-minded man, unstable in all his ways. (James 1:7–8, NASB)

6) Harm to self and delaying your journey. Jealous and looking to others to compare.

What did you think as you traveled down the river? Did you see houses where you imagined happy families? Did you feel that you are being treated unfair? Did you want what you see and don't have? Did you see problems of others?

> But if you have bitter jealousy and selfish ambition in your heart do not be arrogant and so lie against the truth. (James 3:14, NASB)

> You adulteresses, do you not know that friendship with the world is hostility toward God? Therefore, whoever wishes to be a friend of the world makes himself an enemy of God. (James 4:4, NASB)

Were the shores sloped and casual or steep and sharp? When you are ready, there is still no way to climb. You are trapped by the walls of a canyon. The river has dug its path. You are exhausted and at the mercy of the current and terrain of the land. Are the birds provided for, trees growing strong?

7) Ask God and the Holy Spirit for direction. He may not show you the whole trip but will give you

your next step. He will also show you to reach solid ground.

> And in that day you will ask Me no question. Truly, truly I say to you, if you shall ask the Father for anything, He will give it to you in My name. Until now you have asked to nothing in My name; ask and you will receive, that your joy may be full. (John 16:23–24, NASB)

Where is God taking you? Are you fighting the travel, the path that will take you to the point you can get out? Can you feel the ground beneath you yet or stand up yet? What is the timing of the trip? If you try to get out, will it be too soon? Is there a better exit coming?

8) God knows the timing. Seek wisdom for the answers, and be patient waiting success will come.

> Cease striving and know that I am God; I will be exalted among the nations, I will be exalted in the earth. (Psalm 46:10, NASB)

> Call to Me and I will answer you, and I will tell you great and mighty things, which you do not know. (Jeremiah 33:3, NASB)

God wants you to succeed and is there to help.
In applying the picture of our trip down the river, we are looking for tools to succeed in problem solving. Sometimes

the only solution is to wait out the problems and be carried by God through His protection.

You gain wisdom and skills when faced with an overwhelming problem. Pastor TD Jakes said during one of his broadcasts (paraphrased from TBN broadcast October 2019), "Your problem is the bridge to your success. You cannot avoid problems. Problems bridge us to the other side."

What problem-solving skills do you have to succeed? Look for solutions that are provided. Is there a shore to step on or a walk you can take? Can you clearly see the path when you leave the current problem? Your challenges are designed to help you build skill and better judgment. Problems can come from choices we make or someone else imposed on us. No matter the cause, there is something that can be learned. Looking for answers is an action related to attitudes. We go where we choose to go, (1) to the dark, you become a victim again, or (2) to God's provision, being thankful, and (3) in always learning from the experience, you survived.

Learn a new skill of how to give someone information and still not own their problem. Your life may be an inspiration and motivation for someone else to reach for a better life. God uses the Holy Spirit to speak to His people. Know that others are watching you and can see the flame. It may be the spark to start a new flame in them.

> For this reason, I remind you to fan into flame the gift of God, which is in you through the laying on of my hands.
> (2 Timothy 1:6, NIV)

Not everyone wants to set goals for growing and change. Your energy is limited. Problem solving for others can be challenging and depressing. You may lose interest in your own goals for a better future after using your energy to support others. Learn how to be a benefit to others and stay a benefit to yourself and the call God has for you.

Consider Only the Next Step. Be Strategic in Your Planning.

You survived the trip downstream (the last problem) and can now touch bottom again. What next?

Look at steps and new problems that need to be met by considering a picture of the river.

1) Make an assessment of where you are.

You still need to get to the other side of the river. You find that you still have not reached your new country (your long-term goal) and are now on the wrong side of the river. There are valleys, mountains, and hills to climb in your promised land. You see them in the distance and need to get to the right shore.

You must get back in the dangerous river and face a variety of problems and obstacles. You are going to have to get wet again and know the water is cold. You know that the river was designed by God, and you must navigate across river to move into a better life. The river will be a challenge and is designed to discourage you or even stop your success.

God is with you as you enter the water again. Reentering to face the problem is temporary and a realigning time, cleaning up the path to a better foundation for the future.

Not every trip across the river can be smooth. Backtracking to take a better and safer route may be necessary. Keep your vision and goal in mind when you need to make a new strategy.

Problems may come when you think you successfully crossed a rock in your river.

You may find out later the rock had moss on it. The step you took a few days ago or last week, you have to do over. You can't dig up the moss-covered rock. You cannot ignore the rock because it is a foundation rock needed in your plan. You just have to redo your step on in the plan.

Assignment 1

Complete A or B. Pick the style you would to use in tracking your next step.

    A. Write out your goals for the next six months. Break down your plan, things you need to do first, second, so forth until you reach the finished goal.

Write down the time line to complete each step.

If possible, find someone you can trust and who will encourage you in reaching your goals.

Write down how you are going to award yourself when you finish the journey. (Note: If your goal is to finish a class, this is given to you. Choose to reward yourself with something you can only give yourself. Your reward can be simple or big. New outfit? Day trip? Eating out? Day off to just rest? See a movie? Your favorite ice cream or candy bar?)

Your goals are the stones you need to reach the other shore. Your plan may get you wet in the river. Try to develop a plan to step on the rocks that will keep you dry.

Prior to your last stone in the river start to set your next goal for a new achievement. There is a mountain to climb and valleys to cross. Where are you going to go in your new adventure?

    B.   Set daily and weekly goals.

From the chapter "Is Your Tortoise Shell Too Small?" look at your list of "Dream Big." Choose a "Dream Big" to work on.

Set daily, weekly, and yearly goals to reach the *dream*.

To reach the other side of the river consider what needs to be your first step. Where are you going to place your foot? What large or medium rocks are there to step on? How wide will the step need to be and how deep is the water around the rock you have selected to step on to?

Write down the steps needed to overcome today's problems.

Write down the steps needed to overcome week's problems.

Look at the problems you face. Are some of the problems more pressing to solve?

Must you step on one rock problem before you can step on the next rock?

What order do you need to solve the problems? Is one or two more important than the rest of the problems?

Now that you have your plan, step into the river, the first rock.

The hardest step to move into a future can be taking the first step.

You may not know how to get to the other side. The other steps will come after you chose to get wet in the river.

Setting goals? What goals have you set: family time, school, work, housing, recreational, self-improvement, helping others, volunteers, age, life, spiritual, travel, writing, creating, art, music, supporting others, mentoring, coaching, challenging, solving problems, strengthening, softening, teaching, forgetting pain, redesigning, speaking, inspiriting, laughing.

Learn the skill. What you learned or have gained experience in is *strategic planning*. Business and private people use strategic planning to reach an outcome.

Assignment 2

Read from the Bible Numbers 13:25–33. Answer the following questions.

Did God provide a promised land?

If there was a Promised Land, who would be able to enter the land?

Did all the spies enter the promise land? Why or why not?

What were the attitudes of the people who got to have the promise or did not gain the promise?

Can we today derail or delay promises God has given?

Are the promises still ours to take? Can we learn how to become King's Kids and take ownership of what God has promised?

CHAPTER 9

Come to the Beach

Imagine standing on a warm, damp, golden, sand-covered beach. From the warm beach, you can look out upon the beautiful view of the ocean, glittering water stretching beyond the great expanse much farther than your vision and mind can comprehend.

Wiggling your toes, you can feel the comfort of the warm, damp sand and the gentle lapping of salty sea water rinsing your feet.

You came to the beach to pray and think. You need answers to many problems. You are looking for strategic plans, a God-designed plan. How can God help solve financial needs? How do you handle the problem with someone close to you or someone you know? Where is the time to do everything (all seem important) that need to get done? Is there a better life? Why can't you hear from God? Why do you feel stuck? Can God even help you or see you? Are your problems too small for God to notice? Does God even see how badly you are hurting? Why do you feel so confused? Where is God anyway, and will He ever answer?

Looking down at the sand under your feet, you pick up a few single grains of golden sand. You bring them up to look at them very closely. This single piece of sand has a shape of many sides. You may think it represents the problem you are facing today, a many-sided problem that you do not have the answers. You drop the sand pieces and pick up another particle of sand. It is wet. It is different than the other pieces yet still very similar. This piece of sand represents a different problem in your life that also needs your close attention.

The golden beach is filled with thousands of small sand pieces. Each piece of sand with the points and sides and having individual hues of color, some darker, some a lighter gold or white.

If you collect some of the sand, you could make an hour glass. Where did the tiny timepieces of sand come from? The pounding of waves and surf over many years? How far did each piece travel to reach this beach? Is the sand at its final destination or still on a journey? How big was the piece of sand when it started? A large boulder, lava flowing, heating in the center of earth, and cooling to a stone glass when it reached the surface? How much time and effort did it take for this little golden sand grain to reach this point in the beach?

If this single piece of sand started as a boulder, brought slowly to this beach by currents and storms or a lava flow forming into solid rock, what passion or strength of force started the huge mass on a journey to becoming a tiny single piece of sand now under your feet and on this beach? What oversaw the making and direction of a single sand's journey? Did it always have company and travel with the rest of the sand onto the beach? Did the journey include separation from the source and other parts of nature? Did the sand start from the cliffs above the shore and break apart one day falling to be ripped by the sea it had overlooked.

What was the number of challenges and the magnitude of force needed for this small particle to be so warm and wet in your hand or under your feet? The beach you now stand on definitely went through a great journey and has a purpose. There is strength in the number of sand grains working together. One grain under foot would not be noticed. Working together, they move great distances affecting and bringing change to the world.

Looking out over the ocean, you know there are many more sandy beaches, and there is much life within the water.

Your walk on the beach has caused a change in you. Like the sand, your purpose can carry you across oceans or just a few blocks. The steps you take have shifted sand, and its journey may change. A slight change is not noticed by the eye, but a change set the sand to be picked up by a wave and carried to another shore.

In this chapter, you will look at the impact that you can make on the world. Consider how you handle your thoughts. Like the sand on the beach, you arrived at this time and place through your history. When the storms came, you may have been violently moved. You may have had storm damage that caused a costly setback. When you traveled, you encountered others who affected your life, and you affected their life.

The process has taken away sharp edges. You are still on a journey. Your journey will never stop. Think about where you are now and where you would like to be someday. How do you approach thoughts? Look at how God thinks about your value. What do you think He would say is your best trait? What problem is He helping you solve? What does God think when He sees you? You are wonderfully made, and He sees you as His masterpiece.

You will start to look at the world and your life from God's perspective.

> For My thoughts are not your thoughts, neither are your ways My ways, declares the Lord. For as the heavens are higher than the earth, So, are My ways higher than your ways, and My thoughts than your thoughts. (Isaiah 55:8–9, NASB)

> But he who is spiritual appraises all things, yet he himself is appraised by no man. For who has known the mind of the Lord that He should instruct Him? But we have the mind of Christ. (1 Corinthians 2:15–16, NASB)

By studying the word of God and listening to accurate teaching of God's word, you can develop your spirit to recognize the voice of God. The body is your shell to live in with arms and legs. Your soul is the sin nature that wants to rebel. The spirit man is the part that hears and responds to God's voice and seeks to worship God. It seeks the kingdom of heaven.

Make me know Thy ways, O Lord; Teach me Thy paths. Lead me in Thy truth and teach me, for Thou art the God of my salvation. (Psalm 25:4–5, NASB)

You can develop your spirit to hear and respond to problems. You can be led by the Holy Spirit and hear when there may be unforeseen dangers. You can make better informed decision that will be beneficial to your future.

Led by the Spirit or led by the flesh-world-learned way of solving problems.

Assignment: Write down how you handle thoughts, and today solve problems.

These are things or thoughts I am always thinking about and worry about:

These are things or thoughts I sometimes think about and occasionally have concern about:

These are the things or thoughts that I procrastinate on and don't want to meet the challenge. They nag at me:

These are things or thoughts I rarely think about; they are not a priority at this time:

These are the things or thoughts that I never think about. They are just in the background, and I hope will eventually be taken care by events or time:

Through the next week read through the book of Proverbs. There are thirty-one chapters. Each chapter speaks about wisdoms we can have in life. Because there are thirty-one chapters, there are people who choose to read through Proverbs each month, one chapter each day.

In Proverbs, wisdom is the following:

> A wise man will hear and increase in learning, and a man of understanding will acquire wise counsel, The fear of the Lord is the beginning of knowledge; Fools despise wisdom and instruction. (Proverbs 1:5,7, NASB)

Keep a written log of scriptures found in Proverbs that you may want to reread and memorize.

You can learn to handle problems in a Godly way. In learning more of God, you will learn how to encourage yourself in difficult times. You will learn to see answers that may not have been seen before. You can find peace that the world does not have.

> The Lord is my shepherd, I shall not want. He makes me lie down in green pastures; He leads me beside quiet waters. He restores my soul; He guides me in the paths of righteousness for His name's sake. (Psalm 23:1–3, NASB)

> My sheep hear my voice, and I know them, and they follow Me. (John 10:27, NASB)

> And now I commend you to God and to the word of His grace, which is able to build you up and to give you the inheritance among all those who are sanctified. (Acts 20:32, NASB)

> Now we pray to God that you do no wrong; not that we ourselves may appear approved, but that you may do what is right, even though we should appear unapproved. For we can do nothing against the truth but only for the truth. (2 Corinthians 13:7–8, NASB)

Look up and write down peace scriptures: Ecclesiastes 3:8, Isaiah 9:6, Isaiah 66:12, John 14:27, Romans 5:1, Galatians 5:22, Ephesians 2:14, Ephesians 6:15, Philippians 4:7, Colossians 1:20, and Revelation 6:4.

CHAPTER 10

Bless This Mess!

Everyone has challenges. During challenges, some people have more support from family, friends, or community. Others may have found that family, friends, and community are more of a hindrance to reaching higher goals and may even create more problems.

> By wisdom a house is built, and by understanding it is established; and by knowledge the rooms are filled with all precious and pleasant riches. (Proverbs 24:3–4, NASB)

There are lessons in challenges. You start with survival skill. You learn problem solving, your royal rights, and authority as a child of God. If a problem or challenge is handled correctly or mishandled, you still learn from the process. In a success, you have learned how to push through and arrive. A success may not show the details of the process you go through to succeed. In the failure, there are details that can be learned to make you a conqueror. A failure needs to be explored to identify barriers to the success. In the exploration, you can come to a divide in the road. One direction will help you see the walls of resistance. The other direction brings you to a dead end, a place of self-pity where you want to give up because you do not see an out. You give in and become overwhelmed.

You can always choose a direction to overcoming the barriers. You have help that will push you up and over. Through the Holy Spirit of God, you can live a life that is more than daily surviving. You can learn to live as an overcomer and conqueror.

> A wise man is strong, and a man of knowledge increases power. (Proverbs 24:5, NASB)

In life messes, you find strength or defeat. When you have failed, do a treasure to find lessons that identify growth and strength. You are also increasing in wisdom and discernment that you can carry with you to accomplish your bigger assignment. Your destiny and purpose are always moving forward. Not learning from mistakes can keep you from reaching your God purpose. Forget any past mistake that you believe took you on a life detour. God sees the whole journey and knows the perfect place for you to reconnect to the main road. He creates the bends, hills, and U-turns in the road. He sees the overall map and will lead back to your purpose. He takes your human actions and heals, corrects, and puts you back into alignment. He can overcome all the delays and traps that came against your success.

> Finally, be strong in the Lord, and in the strength of His might. Put on the

full armor of God, that you may be able to stand firm against the schemes of the devil. (Ephesians 6:10–11, NASB)

In the process of realignment with God, you learn to trust Him and how to live a new life. You start to understand you are totally forgiven. Through relationship with God, you build strength and understanding of the loving heavenly Father. You learn skills and prepare for larger battles ahead, future battles that today would destroy you. Because they are a part of your future, you will have grown. You are learning how to handle today's challenges. You are continuing to grow in confidence and strength. You are being trained to take on more responsibilities. You can be assured that God is preparing you for the place where you will use the talents and skills. He designed and uniquely created you for the purpose you have to fulfill. In discovering and fulfilling your purpose, you will find a place to live in peace, success, and blessing upon blessing, greater blessings and success that are only found in living and fulfilling your God call.

The journey process is a blessing.

> How great is Thy goodness, which Thou hast stored up for those who fear Thee, Which Thou has wrought for those who take refuge in thee. (Psalm 34:19, NASB)

The journey with God is a process of preparation, a blessing not a curse. You have equipment available to help you reach your destination.

Prepare for the battle. Look at the *full armor* of God that is available for you every day. Armor is something that is to be worn not carried. You are prepared for battle ahead of the fight. With the armor, you are strong in the Lord. Full armor covers the whole body and uses the shield and weapons of a sword to defend.

Assignment

Write out the parts of your armor from Ephesians 6:10–18.

Ephesians 6:

Be strong. Write down verse 10.

Stand firm. Verses 11 and 12.

Able to resist. Verse 13.

Belt of truth. Breastplate of righteousness. Verse 14.

Wherever you go, your feet are covered with gospel and peace. Verse 15.

Your shield is in your hand and moves any direction. It is the faith that stops the attacks before they reach their target. Believe that God's got this and desires for you have every truth and promise He has given. The attacks have no impact. They bounce off your faith and shrivel up under your feet. By faith, you know you already have the victory. Verse 16.

Without salvation, you are not covered by the blood. Verse 17.

You carry power by the sword. It is the word of God. The sword is fluid, moving, and sharp. It is the weapon you use to cut into and destroy your enemy, the weapon to disarm problems. The words of God have power that will defeat in the battle. Verse 17.

Prayer opens the window of heaven and reveals and releases answers. Prayer allows conversation with God. It is a place to learn and also listen. God wants to tell you what is on His heart and show you answers. There is no limit of time in prayer. Prayer reveals and can help you today and tomorrow. Verses 18–19.

David Had Prepared for the Battle

David could not go into battle and fight Goliath with armor and equipment that did not fit. He was offered someone else's war armor but could not use the armor made by man. It was too heavy. Your man-made armor is also to heavy and must be surrendered to make room for the *armor of God*. God designed your armor to fit you perfectly for your war battles.

David got to know God. He had a personal relationship with God. He was a keeper of the sheep in the fields. In Psalms, God says that David was after God's own heart. David took time to know the passion of God. We can get to know the mind of Christ.

> For who has known the mind of the Lord, that He should instruct Him? But we have the mind of Christ. (1 Corinthians 2:16, NASB)

> But seek first His kingdom and His righteousness; and all these things shall be added to you. (Matthew 6:33, NASB)

David took time to wait. He stayed in a quiet place and unseen until God determined it was time to reveal David's gifts. God brought David from the field. He was thought to be a nobody. God knew him and would make him a king. When David was revealed, God chose to have David anointed in public. He announced that David was purposed to be king.

> I delight to do Thy will, O My God; Thy law is within my heart. (Psalm 40:8, NASB)

> Hear my prayer, O Lord, and give ear to my cry; Do not be silent at my tears; For I am a stranger with Thee, A sojourner like all my fathers. (Psalm 39:12, NASB)

David spent time refining his talents and skills.

David's first battle was not to defeat the giant Goliath. He had smaller battles and practiced his slingshot weapons. He was able to accurately hit the target between the eyes because of time spent alone in practice. There is no wasted time if you find that you are alone. God will set you apart to be alone, a place and time to develop your skills. At the end of the battle, David used the giant's own sword to cut off his head.

David knew the battle he had been given was already won. He had confidence that God was with him, and he was prepared to fight. No one else was willing to fight the battle. He went without fear. He had seen in his spirit the defeat of the enemy.

The rest of Saul's armies were afraid of Goliath. David took the talents and equipment God used for training in the quiet time. God supplied the greater. David used the enemy's weapon to destroy the enemy of the country. The stone brought the enemy down. He was already dead. The weapon finished the job as a witness of complete defeat of the enemy.

When you feel alone in your walk, this is not wasted time. God is preparing your spirit and revealing talents. You are in a time to develop skills that He has put within you, talents that He designed to be used, talents that will reveal His goodness and salvation to the world. Your time apart will draw you closer to God. If He is the only person you can share your dreams and desires with, that's okay. He will pull back the curtain at the right time to reveal His plan. You are in a special place and have the opportunity to intimately communicate with and listen for God. He is talking to your spirit. Seeking Him during these quiet times is a privileged time. Your talents are not about you but the kingdom. Your talents and gifts are given to you from God.

You are given the armor of God. You represent and do battle for the kingdom and yourself. In God's army, you have power to release those who have been taken by the enemy. You carry the authority and anointing of the King Himself. You have a covering and carry legal papers. By the king's authority and power, you are commissioned to succeed. In the strategic plan, the outcome of the battle has already been decided. You win!

> Let a man regard us in this manner, as servants of Christ, and stewards of the mysteries of God. In this case, moreover, it is required of stewards that one be found trustworthy. (1 Corinthians 4:1–2, NASB)

Assignment

When have you needed to wait on the Lord?

David was to be king. Discuss how waiting prepared him for his God purpose. David was a relative of Jesus.

Look up in Matthew the scripture that tells about King David being in Jesus's relative.

Look up Isaiah 9:6–7. Who was the prophet Isaiah talking to? Was what he said accurate?

CHAPTER 11

It Takes a Mountain to Climb

In this chapter, you will make the journey to the top of your own mountain. It is steep, and you will make the climb alone. God designed your mountain and named it after you. You do not want to start the climb to face new obstacles and don't want to start your journey. You have become too comfortable with the familiar; you do not want to face the challenges of change. You know of and want a better life, but it is difficult to leave what you know.

The climb up the mountain means there is a road that leads to a better life. You are scared of the future goodness and do not believe you deserve the good and the promises God wants to give to you. Your biggest doubts are not coming from your neighbors or people around you. Your enemy today is yourself. Surely you don't deserve to have anything good. You listen to the voice inside, and it tells you to make the trip.

You have determined that you must take your trip. Life is too difficult to stay. If you don't, you will never see if there is a promised land God created just for you. The answer is on the other side of the mountain.

Today you choose to face your fears and approach the mountain. Taking a long, deep breath, you leave the past behind and make a shaky first step onto the path.

> For now Thou dost number my steps, Thou dost not observe my sin. (Job 14:16, NASB)

Looking at the mountain in front of you, you see it looks huge. You are hidden in its great shadow. You do not know what would happen if you attempt the climb. You do now know the promises God has given you and desire to see the top of the mountain.

God created your mountain and led you to it. You cannot go around it or avoid the trip. You will fail in your climb if you only depend on yourself and not God.

You have your sight set on a better life, but your future is not going to come in one big leap over the mountain. Your new life will only come in the process of making the journey. You will not be able to handle the future that will be given to you without learning what is taught on this mountain named after you.

Every choice you make will take you forward, backward, or off the side of the cliff. Yes, God can catch you if you fall, but there is still disaster, and you will not meet with your divine future.

The slope of the trail is gentle, and you notice the activity of rabbits and sparrows. A monarch butterfly catches your attention as it floats ahead on your path. You want to follow the monarch. There are smells of honey and wild grass. The soft breeze brushes against your cheeks.

There is a bend in the path. It narrows. You continue your walking. Your feet are getting dusty.

> For we walk by faith not by sight. (2 Corinthians 5:7, NASB)

> All the paths of the Lord are lovingkindness and truth to those who keep His covenant and His testimonies. 11) For Thy name's sake, O Lord pardon my iniquity, for it is great. (Psalm 25:10–11, NASB)

Off in the horizon the sun is starting to set. You enjoy the beauty of the colors He has created.

> Therefore, if any man is in Christ, he is a knew creature; the old things passed away; behold new things have come. (2 Corinthians 5:17, NASB)

Vision of the valley. During your walk, you see a valley, and there are some of your coworkers. You did not want to bring them to this mountain. You knew God said to go alone, and you are sure your companions were not trained for this climb. You see them below and the journey they now will be taking. Some will go through deep rivers and over waterfalls; others will walk through a dangerous canyon. One has a companion for the trip to go deep into the dark forest. You see two or three that are standing with armor around their bodies. They are fervent in their battle cries. You hear their voices carried past you and into the heaven and the throne room of God. You realize each of your coworkers are being assigned to the territory they will travel.

You begin to recognize the call and anointing each person is to fulfill. It is different than your mountain climb and the territory you will possess on the other side of the mountain. They are called by God to complete their special purpose. They are training and fulfilling their unique God call with the anointing He gave each one of them. You marvel at the goodness of God and now must continue your journey up the mountain.

> And not only this but he has also been appointed by the churches to travel with us in this gracious work, which is being administered by us for the glory of the Lord Himself, and to show our readiness, 20) taking precaution that no one should discredit us in our administration of this generous gift; 21) for we have regard for what is honorable, not only in the sight of the Lord, but also in the site of men, 22) and we have sent with them our brother whom we have often tested and found diligent in many things, but now even more diligent, because of his great confidence in you. 24) Therefore openly before the churches show them the proof of your love and of our reason for boasting about you. (2 Corinthians 8:19–22, 24, NASB)

The sun has set, and the darkness is making your steps hard to see. At times, you stumble and are not even sure if you are still on the path.

> But I am not silenced by the darkness, nor deep gloom which cover me. (Job 23:17, NASB)

> Behold, I go forward but He is not there, and backward, but I cannot perceive Him; When He acts on the left, I cannot behold Him; He turns on the right, I cannot see Him. But He knows the way I take; When He has tried me, I shall come forth as gold. (Job 23:8–10, NASB)

Through the cold night, you have stumbled your way. You felt alone confused and abandoned by God.

> If I say, "Surely the darkness will overwhelm me, and the light around me will be night, Even the darkness is not dark to Thee, and the night is as bright as the day. Darkness and light are alike to Thee. For Thou didst form my inward parts; Thou dost weave me in my mother's womb." (Psalm 139:11–13, NASB)

The sun begins to rise, and with darkness lifted, you see your way. You have come farther than you thought. You look up, and there is a table set with something lite to eat and a cool brook of fresh running water coming out of carveouts on the path. You are very hungry, and the food is good—sweet fruits and nuts dusted with cinnamon and spices.

> The afflicted shall eat and be satisfied; Those who seek Him will praise the Lord, let your heart live forever. (Psalm 22:26, NASB)

You eat and rest in the warm morning. You drink of the cool water and dream of where the source must be coming from.

> Jesus answered and said to her, "If you knew the gift of God, and who it is who says to you, 'Give Me a drink,' you would have asked Him, and He would have given you living water." (John 4:10, NASB)

You found rest. Taking advantage of the warmth of the sun, you catch a brief nap.

It is only a brief nap, for you are gently awakened by a large being. You are frightened from his size. He speaks softly but with authority. "It is time to leave. You must finish your journey over the mountain. I have some instructions for you. You listen intently, and wait on the Lord's instruction. He will give you provision and wisdom for your journey."

> Then the Lord said to Moses, "Behold, I will rain bread from heaven for you; and the people shall go out and gather a day's portion every day, that I may test them, whether or not they will walk in My instruction." (Exodus 16:4, NASB)

> Jesus said to them, "My food is to do the will of Him who sent Me, and to accomplish His work." (John 4:34, NASB)

> Who is the man who fears the Lord? He will instruct him in the way he should choose. (Psalm 25:12, NASB)

You are told to move quickly, for the time is growing shorter for His last return. There is a job that all who follow Him must complete. The battle will be great, and there will be many who will turn away.

> And He said to them, 'Go into all the world and preach the gospel to all creation. 16 He who has believed and has been baptized shall be saved; but he who has disbelieved shall be condemned. 17 And these signs will accompany those who have believed; in My name they will cast out demons, 18 they will speak with new tongues; they will pick up serpents and if they drink any deadly poison, it shall not hurt them; they will lay hands of the sick and they will recover. (Mark 16:15–18, NASB)

You focus on what has been said. This journey must be important. Picking up a handful of cinnamon nuts and soaking your shirt in the cool water, you start off on the new day. There are many long and dusty miles yet to walk. Your damp shirt dries quickly in the beating sun. Noon is approaching, and you are thirsty again.

The earth under your feet begins to shake. There are high cliffs on your left and a deep canyon to your right. In the turbulence, dirt and small rocks start to fall from above. A terrible loud noise warns you of the danger above. A huge boulder is breaking loose and plummets to where you are standing. You barely run out of its path in time. It throws up dirt and sharp pieces of rock as it falls and stops now on the path behind you. Your way down the mountain is blocked. You can't go back. There is only the path in front of you.

Walking another three or four miles, you begin to think about the near death you just escaped and question what other dangers may lie ahead. You cannot go back and also do not know if the mountain is safe. The ground rumbles under your feet again knocking you off balance.

> For thus says the Lord, "Just as I brought all this great disaster on this people, so I am going to bring on them all the good that I am promising them." (Jeremiah 32:42, NASB)

You pull yourself back up as the earth keeps moving. The earthquakes created a change in the trail in front of you. The pressure that has built up over many years must be released. God is keeping you in peace. After the shaking stops, you see ahead of you there a new opportunity. Two huge trees have fallen over a canyon in the mountain. The dark canyon you were going to climb down is not your only option. You can now cross the canyon by the trees that have fallen.

> For he says, "At the acceptable time I listened to you, and on the day of salvation I helped you; behold now is the acceptable time," behold now is the day of salvation. (2 Corinthians 6:2, NASB)

As you inch your way across the canyon by the trees, you can now see how dark and deep the canyon became. From the top of the cliff, it did not appear that deep. Along the walls of the canyon are sharp, jagged rocks that overhang and force any traveler deeper. You can now see enormous snakes. They are lashing out at each other and consuming anything that enters the path. The attacks are viscous against their own kind as the smell of death rises from the darkness of the canyon. You can hear the echoes of the many who have lost their way in the canyon.

> No temptation has overtaken you but such as common to man; and God is faithful, who will not allow you to be tempted beyond what you are able, but with the temptation will provide the way to escape also, that you may be able to endure. (1 Corinthians 10:13, NASB)

> He delivers me from my enemies; Surely Thou dost lift me above those who rise up against me; Thou dost rescue me from the violent man. (Psalm 18:48, NASB)

The canyon was going to be your route. You did not believe there was another way. In a brief and strong move of the earth, you now have a way of escape.

> I will give thanks to Thee, for I am fearfully and wonderfully made; Wonderful are Thy works, and my soul knows it very well. My frame was not hidden from Thee, When I was made in secret, and skillfully wrought in the depts of the earth. (Psalm 139:14–15, NASB)

You fall asleep in the cover of a cave just as night comes on you again. You rest peacefully through the night.

> In Thee, O Lord, I have taken refuge; Let me never be ashamed; In Thy righteousness deliver me. Incline Thine ear to me, rescue me quickly; Be Thou to me a rock of strength, A stronghold to save me. For Thou art my rock and my fortress; For Thy name's sake Thou wilt lead me and guide me. (Psalm 31:1–3, NASB)

Waking early, you begin your climb. Losing your balance from a missed step, you fall fifteen feet. Now you have torn your clothes and skinned knuckles and knees.

> I will bless the Lord at all times; His praise shall continually be in my mouth. (Psalm 34:1, NASB)

You hear the voice of your visitor you met with yesterday. He tells you that God is your healer and has seen your fall. He is here to wrap your wounds. He has seen your praise of Him and seen your desire to complete the journey. You are trusting in God even when it hurts.

You feel warmth as the visitors touches your shoulder. Healing comes into your body.

> And the prayer offered in faith will restore the one who is sick, and the Lord will raise him up, and if he has committed sins, they will be forgiven him. (James 5:15, NASB)

> Trust in the Lord and do good; Dwell in the land and cultivate faithfulness, delight yourself in the Lord; and He will give you the desires of your heart. (Psalm 37:3–4, NASB)

The visitor leaves. The rest of the day is silent as you make your way up the mountain. You feel the muscles in your legs and back getting stronger. The pain that was in them yesterday was gone. The heaviness of the journey is now easy.

> I have directed you in the way of wisdom; I have led you in upright paths. When you walk, your steps will not be impeded; and if you run, you will not stumble. Take hold of instruction; do not let go. Guard her, for she is your life. (Proverbs 4:11–13, NASB)

> Commit your way to the Lord, trust also in Him, and He will do it. And He will bring forth your righteousness as the light, and your judgement as the noonday. (Psalm 37:5–6, NASB)

As night falls, you smell rain and see the flash of lightning in the distance. The silence you enjoyed all day is now interrupted. The air is thinner, magnifying the sound of thunder clapping through the mountain.

> For He will give His angels charge concerning you, to guard you in all your ways. They will bear you up in their hands lest you strike your foot against a stone. (Psalm 91:11–12, NASB)

> It is good to give thanks to the Lord, and to sing praises to Thy name, O Most High; to declare Thy lovingkindness in the morning and thy faithfulness at night. (Psalm 92:1–2, NASB)

You are carried through the night and find yourself on the other side of the mountain at dawn. Smell the breeze of salty water. God created man in His image. Gave them orders to fulfill and live in the assignment.

> And God blessed them; and God said to them, 'Be fruitful and multiply, and fill the earth, and subdue it; and rule over the fish of the sea and over the birds of the sky, and over every living thing

that moves on the earth. (Genesis 1:28, NASB)

> Be silent before the Lord God! For the day of the Lord is near, For the Lord has prepared a sacrifice, He has consecrated His guest. (Zephaniah 1:7, NASB)

You have made your journey. Your reward is for you and all generations. Remove your shoes, for you know that you are on God's holy ground.

> My foot has held fast to His path; I have kept His way and not turned aside. I have not departed from the command of His lips; I have treasured the words of His mouth more than my necessary food. (Job 23:11–12, NASB)

> Who has performed and accomplished it, calling forth the generations from the beginning. I, the Lord, am the first, and with the last. I am He. (Isaiah 41:4, NASB)

> And just as My Father has granted Me a kingdom, I grant you that you may eat and drink at My table in My kingdom, and you will sit on thrones judging the twelve tribes of Israel. (Luke 22:29–30, NASB)

Assignment

This was a journey story. What have you learned from the journey?

1) Write down your journey as you see it. Where are you on the journey? What do you think is your purpose or assignment?

You did not plan for the downpour. God sent the downpour. It refreshes you.

2) Write down an unexpected event that refreshed you.

FINDING TREASURES IN ASHES

God created the mudslide to move the boulder you could not climb.

3) Write down a problem or obstacle that was moved for you.

God works ahead of you to get through the disaster and the long road.

4) Write down how you have seen something worked out before you had to solve the problem.

Your back pack is full of your tools chosen by God. He equipped you for this trip.

5) Write down the talents given to you from God. How are they going to help you?

Becoming too complacent in one location is a mark of never arriving.

6) Write down how you may improve your walk destiny to fulfill your purpose and assignment.

Don't worry about the provision. God's got this.

7) Write down three scriptures of when God is the provider.

God will hide you in the cliff during a downpour. God will protect you from the scorching sun.

8) Find three scriptures that say God is your protector.

God will carry you. You will be in His glory.

9) Write down a scripture about the throne room of God. What happens in the throne room?

Angels are assigned to you.

10) Write down the scriptures about being able to judge angels.

Your can have conversations with God.

11) Write down three scriptures about the Holy Spirit or praying.

No one can go on your trip. They have their own road to travel. You may pass by a valley when you see them in the distance and can check in by echo, but they may not have the same call. Your paths may be parallel for a time. Your paths may intersect and work together.

12) Write down a list of people you recognize are on a different path. What are the talents that you see in them? Where do you see your paths intersecting or how do your calls complement each other? Why do you think they are going to succeed? How do you show respect for another person's gifts and talents?

To Think About

    A. In January 1986, America and the world witnessed the end of a voyage. It was not the beginning of the journey because months and years of planning and calculations were made prior to the liftoff. The chosen few people making the trip were educated and informed of the risk. With all the knowledge of risk, there was an overwhelming excitement. They chose to go. Many others had made the same trip, and it was now their turn. They made plans to return and speak of the great adventure into space. They had a purpose.

"Future does not belong to the fainthearted, it belongs to the Brave" (President Ronald Reagan's speech, January 28, 1986). In the *Challenger* space tragedy, seven lives were lost.

All of us make our plans. The plans you walk out with God today affect you and future generations (those watching you in the Spiritual or natural children and grandchildren).

> May He give you the desire of your heart and make all your plans succeed. (Psalm 20:4, NIV)

> But the plans of the Lord stand firm forever, the purposes of his heart through all generations. (Psalm 33:11, NIV)

Find Help With Your Walk:

B. Find things that build you up in the Lord. Music may be one of those things. The Father above is watching over you. You may be the only one whom you know wants to move into a better life. You may be the mentor that others are watching.

Amy Grant produced the song "My Father's Eyes" and released in 1979. In 2003, she produced the "I'm Gonna Fly" and released 2008. Zach Williams song "Fear Is a Liar" was released last 2016.

"Fear Is a Liar" song is now being played in some Domestic Violence recover meetings.

There are several ministry radio stations available throughout parts of the world.

C. "Unbelief often clothes itself in 'being smart'. We use cleverness to cover the tracks of our lack of faith." Book: Fresh Faith copywrite 1999, Jim Cymbala, Pastor Brooklyn Tabernacle. 91. Zondervan Publishing House: Grand Rapids, Michigan 49530.

CHAPTER 12

Keep Your Lamp Plugged In

You are not put on this world to be alone. There is found strength if you can plug into a group of people who share your beliefs. If at all possible, make a connection with a supporting ministry group.

> Let us hold fast the confession of our hope without wavering, for He who promised is faithful; and let us consider how to stimulate one another to love and good deeds, not forsaking our own assembling together, as is the habit of some, but encouraging one another, and all the more, as you see the day drawing near. (Hebrews 10: 23–25, NASB)

Note: The next few paragraphs are written to encourage those who are isolated. Please do not skip over the writing. If you are privileged to worship freely, still think about the isolated that must seek God alone. They need our prayers!

Understanding Situations When It May Not Be Possible to Connect

There may be very few believers where you are living. You may be isolated in a country and your only source to connect is through written materials or radio. It is extremely hard to stand believing alone. Not impossible! Continue to use the few resources available. We are praying for you.

You may have been recently rescued from your abuse or chaos. You are beginning the healing and still are not sure if you can trust.

You may live in a neighborhood or attend a school where there is violence in the streets.

You may be the first to believe in your family. Now you are believing for their salvation.

You may be in a foster group home. You may be a shut-in.

You may be in a prison. You may be in a hospital, in a marriage with a nonbeliever.

If this is you, if you can, please write. The support team of "Finding Treasures in Ashes" would like to frequently pray for you. We do not always know who is isolated in the world and needing prayer unless you tell us.

We want to pray and be a light for you.

For those who are privileged to have multiple resources of connection through church and study groups, please be praying for *believers* who are fighting the battle alone.

Keep your lamp plugged in.

You are wanting to grow in your walk with God. You may be a long-time believer, new believer, or may not have made the decision of Jesus.

Any place you are in, your walk is good. The stage of walk that you are in will be strengthened when you tie into a group of like believers. You cannot make the walk alone!

Plugged into a local church or ministry will help keep you on track. Ministry conferences are a good source of material. They are usually seasonal unless you are traveling all over. Ministry conference are like eating out—very enjoyable. You should be plugging into for your weekly meal at a church. You also cannot just eat once a week without starving. Building a time to eat daily will help you to thrive. This includes reading your Bible, praying, and spending time with God alone. When you attend the weekly meeting, there will usually be confirmations of what God has been showing you alone.

Plug your lamp into a Bible-based church. You must be comfortable with the church teaching and the leadership. The church that your extended family attends or friends attend may be the church you want to attend, or the church they attend may not be the church where you are growing the most and most comfortable. Make the choice for you.

Every church has a personality. The pastor may be vocal and loud or quiet and providing a lot of scripture references. The church may have upbeat and modern music or offer hymns with a large choir and organ.

The church has a personality, and you have a personality that will want to match with the church you are most comfortable in attending.

You will want to find a church or study group that *accurately teaches* the Bible and word of God. The main source of teaching has to be Bible-centered.

Your church you choose is to be on what you believe. It will need to be in line with the basic words of salvation through the blood of Jesus found in the Bible.

The Bible beliefs of Holy Spirit, and Speaking in Tongues may be presented different in churches. What do you believe?

We can live with the foundation of the Bible and the major points of salvation without being at war about the

Gifts of the Spirit still active today. You have to make the choice yourself.

This writer does believe in the spirit and gifts for today. I will not argue and abandon anyone who does not believe the same way.

When someone is attending a church or receiving teachings that present the salvation message. As long as a person is presented with Jesus being the only door to the kingdom of God, who am I to argue. The Holy Spirit can move in any church where He is invited. How that manifests in different ways is dependent on a quiet church or not quiet.

A person may be more comfortable at a quiet church and receive from accurate teaching. The Bible is presented in a more traditional way. The Holy Spirit may move that person to a life change.

Attend where you believe you are to attend without judgement. Denominations are that "denominations."

The benefits and the power of the Holy Spirit may be presented at another church. Some may desire to attend where these gifts are more apparent. The music is presented to usher in the people to deep worship. Bible is message is offered and addresses living today and addressing problems through prayer and hearing directions of the Holy Spirit.

You need to choose where you are comfortable. The Holy Spirit will meet you where you are now and place you where you are able to serve. You are always growing and will know in your heart what are the beliefs that are aligned with your beliefs. If you do not agree with 90 percent or better of what is being taught from the leaders, find someplace else. You will never agree 100 percent. Reading the Bible and studying will cause you to think and may be slightly different in how you understand what you read.

Do not attend a church because of the popularity of or personality of the pastor. You may choose to attend where the personality is dynamic, there is also accuracy in Bible teaching.

You also may choose to attend a mega church or smaller church. It depends on what you are comfortable with or sometimes where you are living.

It is importance to attend church or Bible study somewhere. By attending, you are accountable to the group, and they are accountable to you. Plug in someplace where you continue to grow. When you are a leader, be accountable to another leader or mentor.

Having a Personal Relationship

Seek a personal relationship with God. He desires to spend time with you every day. Some of you may have a child, spouse, or pet that greets you at the door. They want to see and talk with you. They want to share the day they have had.

God is the same. We were created in His image. We were created to spend time with Him.

God created humans to be with Him. We are created to worship.

> As the deer pants for streams of water, so my soul pants for you, O God. My soul thirsts for God, for the living God. When can I go and meet with God? (Psalm 42:1–2, NIV)

Job was declared a fearless and righteous man by God (Job chapters 1 and 2).

Moses was said to be the friend of God (Exodus 33:11).

David's relationship was written as in pursuit of God. "A man after my own heart" (Acts 33:22).

Abraham was a man of faith (Hebrews 11:8).

Rahab was a prostitute and a relative of Jesus. (Hebrews 11:31, Matthew 1:5)

Esther was an orphan called for a purpose—to save the Jewish people (Book of Esther).

You are valuable to God and His ministry at any age.

The righteous will flourish like a palm tree, they will grow like a cedar of Lebanon; planted in the house of the Lord, they will flourish in the courts of our God. They will still bear fruit in old age, they will stay fresh and green, proclaiming, "The Lord is upright; his is my Rock, and there is no wickedness in him" (Psalm 92:12–15, NIV).

Uses your gifts and talents within the Body of Christ.

Many churches have extended programs: children's church, senior or widow's grief programs, support groups for single parents, singles again, youth groups, food banks.

Midweek services or Bible studies may be offered, women's and men's individual prayer during the week, or missionary events, luncheons, and outreaches.

Your Community Needs You

In the community, there may be volunteer opportunities: Christmas or Easter baskets for kids in foster care, outreaches for retirement, shut-ins, or hospitals, support for homeless shelter or domestic violence, crisis pregnancy centers, food banking, after-school programs, and poverty neighborhoods, or overseas missions and ministries.

Consider carefully what you may be able to help. Your talents and gifts from God are a match somewhere. You may assist in an area for a short or longer time. Your gifts will be developed and your understanding of God will grow when you are serving. There are many choices and not all ministry opportunities are for you. You may care about many areas. What is the area that stands out? Where does your passion for helping tug deeply every time the subject or ministry is mentioned? Example: (1) When you hear about the prison outreach program, it gets your attention, and you think, "I can put together boxes of support or go to the prison with the leader who go." (2) When the church ask for volunteers to help with little kids nursery, you are not interested, but when they ask for volunteers for youth and teens, you think, "Teens can talk. It would be exciting to help lead a teen to know Christ."

If you have experienced trauma, God may use this experience to help others. You may have lost a child and can now help others who go through the same loss.

Do not move into ministry, volunteering before you have knowledge of are on the road to learning of who you are in Christ. If you are still too wounded and raw with the trauma, it can (1) cause great damage to you and reinjuring of you, and (2) when you are still too fragile and hurting, you will only end up hurting others. Volunteering helps in your healing only when you are over some of the trauma. It takes time to heal, and volunteering is not a substitute to make yourself feel good instead of addressing the pain.

Be Accountable

You cannot be a volunteer or in ministry or leadership without being accountable to God and providing your talents as a service to God. You will not always be recognized by men but will always be recognized by God. He will observe how you use the talents He gave you. He will promote you or give you more talents when you have been a good steward to Him first.

Second: Provide your services under the care a ministry leader or leader where you are a volunteer. Striking out on your own can be dangerous. In some areas of ministry or outreach, you can even lose your life if you are not with a group of accountable from the leadership. You can also get into legal problems if you try to serve in an area that is not appropriate for you or you are not equipped to serve.

Leadership in your church or ministry of volunteering is able to provide oversite and training.

God gave you talents. Start where you are plugged in.

Stay plugged in to keep growing as a believer. You will find encouragement from like believers.

Assignment

Where are you interested in serving?
Why do you believe this is a good place for you to serve?
Who would you call to ask questions about serving in the area of interest?
What skills can you provide for service?
What talents do you believe God has given you?

CHAPTER 13

This Card Is for Me

As a child of the King, the Most Holy God, you can enter God's *throne room*. You are precious and royal in God's family. Bible scriptures are a love letter to God's people. They provide direction wisdom and revelations about the personality and character of God. You can open the Bible and find the cards of love written to you. You will find acceptance, wisdom, and instruction within the words of God.

This chapter will look at the character of God and who you are as a child of God. You are the child of a fair, faithful, and giving king. You are royalty and have all the rights to spend time with God the Father. By asking, you can at any time enter into His heavenly throne room.

The throne room of God is a real place.

> And I heard a loud voice from the throne, saying, "Behold, the tabernacle of Tod is among men, and He shall dwell among them, and they shall be His people, and God Himself shall be among them, and He shall wipe away every tear

from their eyes; and there shall no longer be any death; there shall no longer be any mourning, or crying, or pain; the first things have passed away." (Revelation 21:3–4, NASB)

Righteousness and justice are the foundation of your throne; love and faithfulness go before you, blessed are those who have learned to acclaim you, who walk in the light of your presence, O Lord. They rejoice in your name all day long; and they exalt you in your righteousness; for you are their glory and strength and by our favor you exalt our horn. (Psalm 89:14–17, NIV)

If then you have been raised up with Christ, keep seeking the things above, where Christ is seated at the right hand of God. (Colossians 3:1, NASB)

What does "ask of God" mean? Getting to know the character of God will help in building your faith. God is a God of love and wants the best for you. Hopefully you are now learning that God loves you and is not wanting to punish you. The world may cause you problems that you can ask God to help you with. People may come against you. You can learn how to handle people's relationships with greater skill and wisdom. God will not snap His fingers and instantly fix your world. He desires to build a relationship with you and will help you endure as you learn to trust Him.

> And in that day you will ask Me no question. Truly, truly I say to you, if you shall ask the Father for anything, He will give it to you in My name. Until now you have asked for nothing in My name, ask, and you will receive, that your joy may be full. (John 16:23–24, NASB)

> In the time of my favor I will answer you, and in the day of salvation I will help you. (Isaiah 49:8a, NIV)

> If the world hates you, you know that it has hated Me before it hated you. (John 15:18, NASB)

The idea of God being a loving Father may be new. I pray that your trust for the heavenly Father has increased as you made your journey through the workbook. Building a new healthier relationship with God takes action on your part. It is like building a relationship with anyone you want to know better.

There is a love note from God to you each day. He is waiting for you to open His note to you. This is one of the ways God will speak to you. You cannot get to know someone's heart if you only look at a picture of them each day. From a picture, you cannot know and hear someone's voice. A picture cannot tell you what the person is thinking or passionate about. The person in the picture may look attractive to you, but you really don't know if the beauty is a façade that hides someone who is cold.

The Character of God

With praise and the word, we worship our King and recognize His attributes.

1) We are made to worship Him.

> Let them praise His name with dancing; Let them sing praises to Him with timbral and lyre. (Tambourine and Harp) For the Lord takes pleasure in His people, He will beautify the afflicted ones with salvation. Let the godly ones exult in glory. Let them sing for joy on their beds. Let the high praises of God be in their mouth, and a two-edged sword in their hand. (Psalm 149:3–5, NASB)

The double-edged sword is a representative of the word and our praises.

> But an hour is coming, and now is, when the true worshipers shall worship the Father in spirit and truth; for such people the Father seeks to be His worshipers. God is spirit and those who worship Him must worship in spirit and in truth. (John 4:23–24, NASB)

2) As a child of the King, we give glory to His name. You are able to see His glory!

> I will give thanks to Thee, O Lord my God, with all my heart, and will glorify Thy name forever. (Psalm 86:12, NASB)

3) God's desire is for you to be in His presence and come to Him in His throne room.

> I am my beloved and His desire is for me. (Song of Songs 7:10, NASB)

> But you when you pray, go into your inner room, and when you have shut your door, pray to your Father who is in secret, and your Father who sees in secret will repay you. (Matthew 6:6, NASB)

Notice that Matthew 6:6 writes "*when* you pray," *not* "*if* you pray."

God desires to be with you, and He wants you to come into His presence even "more" than you want to be in with Him. You enter to talk with God. You can worship Him, praise and dance before the most high God.

4) He heals: He brings you through all the pain and life sorrows. He is worthy of our praise.

> You turned my wailing into dancing; you removed my sackcloth and

clothed me with joy, that my heart may sing your praises and not be silent. Lord my God, I will praise forever. (Psalm 30 11–12, NIV)

5) He makes your life new. He gives you a new beginning and erases the past.

And their sins and their lawless deeds I will remember no more. (Hebrews 10:17, NASB)

6) We may also bring our request, and He will honor us and He hears us.

Ask and it shall be given to you; seek, and you shall find; knock, and it shall be opened to you. For everyone who asks receives, and he who seeks finds, and to him who knocks it shall be opened. (Matthew 7:7–8, NASB)

He hears you and wants to meet your needs. God wants you to come to Him and ask. If you wanted to borrow the car from your earthly father, you would need to ask. Your heavenly Father also wants to hear your voice. If He fulfilled all your needs and wants before you ask, how would you ever learn that He is your provider?

7) He is a good and loving God.

And I will make them and the places around My hill a blessing, and I will cause showers to come down in their season; they will be showers of blessings. (Ezekiel 34:26, NASB)

The Lord has made known His salvation; He has revealed His righteousness in the sight of the nations. He has remembered His lovingkindness and His faithfulness to the house of Israel; All the ends of the earth have seen the salvation of our God. (Psalm 98:2–3, NASB)

8) He is your inheritance.

And everyone who has left houses or brothers or sister or father or mother or children or farms for My name's sake, shall receive many times as much, and shall inherit eternal life. (Matthew 19:29, NASB)

Surely goodness and lovingkindness will follow me all the days of my life. And, I will dwell in the house of the Lord forever. (Psalm 23:6, NASB)

Ask of the Father. Go and seek out where the Fathers is located. Knock on the door, and He will open the door to you.

9) He is a just and fair God.

For the word of the cross is to those who are perishing foolishness, but to us who are being saved it is the power of God. For it is written, "I will destroy the wisdom of the wise, and the cleverness of the clever I will set aside." For since in the wisdom of God the world through its wisdom did not come to know God, God was well-pleased through the foolishness of the message preached to save those who believed. (1 Corinthians 1:18–19, 21, NASB)

10) He is faithful to hear you.

And all things you ask in prayer, believing, you shall receive. (Matthew 21:22, NASB)

11) He is approachable. He answers when you are in distress. He does not judge but loves.

And behold, there was a woman in the city who was a sinner; and when she learned that He was reclining at the table in the Pharisee's house, she brought an alabaster vial of perfume, and standing behind Him at His feet, weeping, she began to wet His feet with her tears, and kept wiping them with the hair of her head, and kissing His feet, and anointing them with the perfume. (Luke 7:37–38, NASB)

> From my distress I called upon the Lord; The Lord answered me and set me in a large place. (Psalm 118:5, NASB)

> Blessed is a man who perseveres under trail; for one he has been approved, he will receive the crown of life, which the Lord has promised to those who love Him. (James 1:12, NASB)

12) He catches and holds all your tears. You stay close to His heart. He doesn't forget you. Your tears are important to Him, or He would not notice and keep them. He feels your hurt with you.

> Record my misery; list my teas on your scroll—are they not in your record? (Psalm 56:8, NIV)

> For the Lamb in the center of the throne shall be their shepherd, and shall guide them to springs of the water of life; and God shall wipe every tear from their eyes. (Revelation 7:17, NASB)

13) He sets the captive free.

> Those who sow in tears shall reap with joyful shouting. He who goes to and from weeping carrying his bag of seed, shall indeed come again with a shout of joy, bringing his sheaves with him. (Psalm 126:5–6, NASB)

> This is what the Lord says: "Restrain you voice from weeping and your eyes from tears, for your work will be rewarded." Declares the Lord. 'They will return from the land of the enemy. (Jeremiah 31:16, NIV)

14) He sees you. You are not alone in the battle. God shows His power through your walk.

> Hear the world of the Lord, you who tremble at His word: "Your brothers who hate you, who exclude you for My name's sake," Have said, "Let the lord be glorified, that we may see your joy." But they will be put to shame. (Isaiah 66:5, NASB)

> Let your light shine before men in such a way that they may see your good works, and glorify your Father who is in heaven. (Matthew 5:16, NASB)

> Sing to the Lord, all the earth; Proclaim good tiding of His salvation from day to day. Tell of His glory among the nations, His wonderful deeds among all the peoples. For great is the Lord, and greatly to be praised; He also is to be feared above all gods. (1 Chronicles 16:23–25, NASB)

15) He planned for you.

> For you created my inmost being; you knit me together in my mother's womb. (Psalm 139:13, NIV)

> "For I know the plans I have for you," declares the Lord, "plans to prosper you and not to harm you, plans to give you hope and a future." (Jeremiah 29:11, NIV)

> Being confident of this, that he who began a good wok in you will carry it on to completion until the day of Christ Jesus. (Philippians 1:6, NIV)

> The counsel of the Lord stands forever, The plans of His heart from generation to generation. (Psalm 33:11, NASB)

16) He is forgiving.

> And whenever you stand praying, forgive, if you have anything against anyone; so that your Father also who is in heaven may forgive you your transgressions. (Mark 11:25, NASB)

> For His anger is but for a moment, His favor is for a lifetime; Weeping may last for a night, but a shout of joy comes in the morning. (Psalm 30:5, NASB)

17) He will provide guidance.

> Let no one say when he is tempted, "I am being tempted by God;" for God cannot be tempted by evil, and He Himself does not temp anyone. (James 1:13, NASB)

> But when He, the Spirit of truth, comes, He will guide you into all the truth; for He will not speak on His own initiative, but whatever He hears, He will speak; and He will disclose to you what is to come. (John 16:13, NASB)

> Many are the plans in a person's heart, but it is the Lord's purpose that prevails. (Proverbs 19:21, NIV)

> He restores my soul; He guides me in the paths of righteousness. (Psalm 23:3, NASB)

> For such is God, Our God forever and ever; He will guide us until death. (Psalm 48:14, NASB)

Assignment

Use any resource you may have. Look up and write down scriptures where God is known to be:

18) Provider for you.

Philippians 4:19
2 Corinthians 9:12
Deuteronomy 15:6
Acts 20:35
Psalm 9:18
Psalm 69:33

19) He is a teacher.

> Teach me Thy way, O Lord; I will walk in Thy truth; Unit my heart to fear Thy name. (Psalm 86:11, NASB)

20) He is wise and gives wisdom.

> But if any of you lacks wisdom, let him ask of God, who gives to all men generously and without reproach and it will be given to him. (James 1:5, NASB)

21) He is honest. Write down the scriptures that say God cannot lie.

22) He answers your questions.

Proverbs 24:26.
Psalm 118:5

23) He is a protector.

> And now, my daughter, do not fear. I will do for you whatever you ask, for my people in the city know that you are a woman of excellence. (Ruth 3:11, NASB)

> Every word of God is tested; He is a shield to those who take refuge in Him. (Proverbs 30:5, NASB)

24) Where does scriptures say that "He is strong, wise and all knowing"?

25) Find the scripture: He knows you intimately. He knows the number of hairs on your head. He has numbered your days.

26) He gives you seed to sow. He wants to bless you. Write down the scriptures about the seeds He will give you. How is the production of seed He gives measured? What are the seeds?

He provides water for the seeds you have planted.

> Ask rain from the Lord at the time of the spring rain—The Lord who makes the storm clouds; And He will give them shower of rain vegetation in the field to each man. (Zechariah 10:1, NASB)

27) Before God made His creation, there was no time. Time was introduced for man's benefit.

Look up Genesis 1, about time and creation, and Revelations 22, regarding time.

Also look up and read the full chapter of John 1. In John 1, who did it say was at the creation? In John 1:15, who is the person whom John said *"he saw coming,"* and John also said he was talking about before *he came*?

God said He is the beginning and the end, "Alpha and Omega." Look up the scripture reference. What does it mean to be the "Alpha and Omega"?

28) He has created a place for you. He wants you with Him forever and ever.

What does Revelation 22:5 say about time? What does Revelation 22:5 say about you?

> And there shall no longer be any night; and they shall not have need of the light of a lamp nor the light of the sun, because the Lord God shall illumine them; and they shall reign forever and ever. (Revelation 22:5, NASB)

29) He called you to be a voice for Him to tell others that He loves them and wants to save them.

Write down how you may today and this week be a voice for God.

30) He is the designer and creator of a flawless plan. How is His plan flawless?

CHAPTER 14

Blessed to Succeed, Succeed to Bless

Be a blessing to others and be a blessing to yourself.

Many of our adventures and experiences we are surrounded by other people—family, friends, acquaintances, coworkers. Some of these people are in our life for a short period, others are there for a lifetime. Does that mean that each of these people are to go on the next life journey or spiritual journey with us?

Let's examine Bible history. Who made the journey, who went on to fulfill their divine destination alone? What were the assignments that required the individual to travel alone? What was the support team of those that remained with the person in their story?

Abraham and Moses were positioned to walk out their divine purposes. They made major mistakes. Mistakes will not stop your destiny.

Abraham

God had a divine assignment for Abraham. Did Abraham travel alone? God had told Abraham to leave his father and family and go into an unknown place. When Abraham started his journey, he did not know where he was going. He just left the land he knew and went by the direction of God. Abraham did compromise the direction of God by not leaving his whole family. He chose to take his nephew Lot with him.

> The Lord said to Abram, "Leave your country, your people and your father's household and go to the land I will show you. I will make you a great nation and bless you; I will make your name great, and you will be a blessing." So, Abram left, as the Lord had told him and Lot went with him. (Genesis 12:1–2, 4, NASB)

This compromise, of taking Lot with him, caused problems in the walk that Abraham was to take. His life was being blessed in numbers, and also the number of Lot's family were increasing. The land would not support both growing populations, and arguments between the workers of Lot and Abraham began. Abraham was a peacemaker and gave Lot the first choice of land. The blessings were on Abraham and his assignment.

Lot chose the land that he believed was well watered and a garden. The blessing was on Abraham. The Bible later picks up the history where Lot and his family moved into Sodom and Gomorrah, a place where God was not found.

Lot and his family were being warned by two angels to leave the place of chaos and destruction. God destroyed the land that Lot had; though, Lot thought, with his natural eyes, was the better land.

Abraham was told by God that Sodom and Gomorrah would be destroyed. Abraham pleads for mercy for the people. God would destroy the towns but save Abraham's relative, Lot.

Abraham finally completed the assignment to leave his family in order to complete the assignment God had given him. God is a God of second and more chances. Abraham had sacrificed by breaking all ties to his natural family and received a promise from God that he would be the father of many and of a nation.

Abraham had no children. Again, tried to fulfill the promise of God through his human efforts, after listening to the human reasons of his wife, Abraham takes a maid and fathers a child. This child was not a perfect plan of God. It would take faith to father the child God had planned, a child from the old and unproductive womb of his wife. This lack of faith and taking the human approach to create a child caused friction with his wife, Sarah, and the maid Hagar.

The child born to Hagar and Hagar become victims not because of something Hagar did wrong but because of the poor choices of Abraham and Sarah. The mother and child were sent to the desert with limited food and water. Hagar, as a victim, cried out to God. She was emotionally hurt and physically hurt. God stepped in and did not allow Ishmael and Hagar to continue to suffer. Ishmael and Hagar lives would not be punished for others' wrongs. Ishmael and Isaac, half-brothers, would always be at war. Abraham left gifts to his other children when he was alive. He gave everything to Isaac when he died. Note: The brothers Ishmael and

Isaac did come together to bury their father. (Abraham was buried next to his first wife, Sarah.)

Abraham had an assignment to get alone with God, separate himself for the purpose of bringing in a new chosen people. From Abraham came Isaac. Abraham first did not walk by faith and took his nephew Lot with him. Abraham also did not live by faith and took the maid Hagar to father a child. Each time his choice costs a human price.

At some point, Abraham learned to walk by faith. He is called the father of many. He believed the word of God. Again, Abraham had an assignment to separate himself from the servants that would travel with him. He and his son Isaac would only go to the top of the mountain to make a sacrifice on the altar to the Lord. Abraham's faith is written about in Hebrews 11.

What would have happened if Abraham had not learned to walk by faith? What if he had taken his servants with him to the mountain for sacrifice? He could have reasoned in his humanness that they were needed to carry the wood or watch for dangers of the mountain. Would the servants have been killed prior to getting to the top of the mountain? Would the servants try to stop the child from being killed? Would they have tried to talk Abraham out of the God plan?

Abraham had learned to follow the direction of God with every detail. It was only Abraham and Isaac who went to the top of the mountain. And it was Abraham and Isaac who received the provision of the sacrifice ram found in the thicket of thorns. Even Isaac had questions of where was the sacrifice. Abraham answered that God would provide but was prepared to know that God would make the promise come true that he had heard. Abraham knew that if God said he would be the father of many, he would become the father of many. Even if Isaac died.

Your purpose and destiny cannot be stopped.

Moses

Moses was born into a Hebrew family at the time that he would have been killed by the pharaoh just for being a Hebrew baby. His mother made plans to have her son placed outside of the home. He made the journey alone into the Pharaoh's castle and became the adopted son of the daughter to Pharaoh.

Moses's destiny could not be stopped. God had chosen the child to free the captives. Moses's mother became a key to the plan when she used wisdom and gave up her son. She would not know until many years later that her son would save the slaves from the pharaoh. God positioned her to be a nursemaid for the child, speaking life into the child as he grew.

Moses was born into destiny with an assignment for leading the Hebrew people out of captivity. He had an assignment at birth to be born at a specific time and place to fulfill his assignment. Moses came to a point in his life that he had to make a decision. Would he continue to live in a life of adopted luxury or would he seek the road that led to his assigned destiny?

Moses made mistakes. He killed a man and in fear ran to the wilderness. His mistakes did not stop his assigned destiny. Within this unknown land, he sought after and found his assignment. This was an alone time and discovery time. Moses received direct words from God and still doubted that he could complete the assignment. Moses questioned God, speaking his feelings of being inadequate. God gives us our assignment for purpose. It is through God, not our own strength, that we fulfill our purpose. After seeking God and many years, Moses returned to the place where he would fulfill his birth purpose.

God gave him a help person who would speak for him, his brother Aaron. This help person also became a hindrance to Moses in leading the people. Aaron was not the one with the assignment. He compromised when the people were in the wilderness, allowing the people to create a golden calf, false God, a history they had learned and been captive too.

What we can learn from the relationship of Aaron and Moses is stay true to your God assignment. Moses was in his assigned place to seek the face of God, receiving the direction of God and at that time the ten commandments that the people would live by. In Exodus 3–4, you can read these events.

1) Seek God for direction. Your assignment will bless others, and you will receive blessing in the process.

Moses was seeking God and was granted the right to be hidden in the cliff of the mountain as God revealed Himself.

2) You may fulfill your assignment with few supporters. God will bring you help as needed.

In order for Moses to be able to lead the Hebrew people out of captivity, he traveled alone to a new land and spent many years in the desert until returning to become the leader of the Hebrew people.

We need to learn tools. Like Moses and Abraham, they learned that they could not take everyone with them. Both went to the top of a mountain. Moses went alone, and Abraham took his only heir to the kingdom. God would use his heir to multiply Abraham's seed and fulfill the promise God gave. Abraham and his son Isaac both were given a purpose.

You also have a purpose in being born when you were born. There is an enemy who has tried to destroy your purpose. Your God-designed purpose still is active. Nothing you have done and nothing that has been done to you can destroy the purpose and call God has put on your life.

Explore and discover your God purpose.

What have you seen you have skills in doing? What talents do you have?

What do you enjoy doing? This is a hint to your God purpose.

Bless others but also take care of yourself.

In the purpose God has designed for your life also may be the area of biggest struggles. Your purpose, talents, and calling are designed to enhance the kingdom of God and will also bring blessings to you and people around you. Given your purpose is designed to move the God kingdom forward and help others you are to meet; it is the same reason that your biggest fight may to be make progress. Distractions and problems hinder your progress. Opposing forces to the kingdom of God do not want your gift to influence others. A child that has a call on their life may be stopped in that calling if you first can be stopped in your progress.

Are you complaining a lot about how others use your time but are not setting limits? Do you complain to others and involve others in your whining? Are you negative and always giving a negative report about the others you help? Why do you help if you complain after you have provided a help? How hard do you have to push back when you say no? Can you say no and stick to the no, or do you allow others to talk you into things you don't want to do? Do others rob you of your time?

Do you respect your time enough to protect the time you need? Does God want you to spend more time with Him? Do you spend more of your time helping and fellowshipping with others or do you allow others to rob the time you should be using to talk to God?

Where is your prayer time? Where are you being refilled, your church services? Are you in a good church service with excellent pastors? Are you in a support group?

Who is your support team? Who is the person who you can be your best and worth with? Who do you give more to but who never give back? What are the lopsided relations that you participant in?

Setting goals? What goals have you set: family time, school, work, housing, recreational, self-improvement, helping others, volunteers, age, life, spiritual, travel, writing, creating, art, music, supporting others, mentoring, coaching, challenging, solving problems, strengthening, softening, teaching, forgetting pain, redesigning, speaking, inspiriting, laughing.

We have an assignment on our life. The assignment may take us away from those who would be negative and hinder us from the assignment that God wants to fulfill. They may be good people and even may be family. They also may be stopping us from moving into the next level of our assignment.

(Do not use God as an excuse to be negligent and abandon children and spouses. God has a voice that will line up with the Bible.)

Husbands, love your wives, just as
Christ loved the church and gave himself

> up for her to make her holy, cleansing her by the washing with the water through the word. (Ephesians 5:25, NASB)
>
> Fathers, do not exasperated your children; instead, bring them up in the training and instruction of the Lord. (Ephesians 6:4, NASB)

How many can you carry into the next phase of where you need to go? By doing a good thing, it may be good, but it is not the God thing. There are three levels of God's plan: good, better, and best. God may allow us to walk in the good plan for a while. We then learn the better plan of His promises, and finally we learn the best plan for the calling on our life—the divine plan that God called us to. Where can you reach the most people with the best quality of service to the people you are assigned to?

What energy does it take to carry others with you? Are you using all your faith to support others (neighbors, extended family) who should be learning to walk in their own plan of God? Are you being hindered in your plan and by assisting others who continue to stay stuck? If so, you are hindering them from growing up in God and have become the source their faith. When you continue to allow others to look at you to solve all their problems, you are getting something. Are you walking in pride, enabling, using them as an excuse to avoid the prayer time, reaching your God purpose goals, allowing others to fill your lonely spaces?

Some people are natural at helping, and that is their calling. It also takes a balance to learn how much to help and how much to give. Giving may be for a season. When is the time to allow someone to do the problem solving on their own? When is the time that you are giving more energy and prayer to solve other people's problems and not moving into exploring the greater plan God has for your life?

It is a tough call especially when it involves family or people you have been close to for many years. Examine your faith level. How do you feel when you see the divine plan of God for your life? Do you feel comfortable sharing your plans that God has given you with the people you are around? Do they support you or are they negative to the plan that you believe God wants for you? When you are with someone, how do you feel when you leave that person?

God has put you on this earth to help and reach people. But not every person can be a permanent person in your assignment. It is a discerning time to weigh the relationships you have and determine to what level you are to allow people to be in your life.

Abraham learned how to let go of his nephew Lot. These are not easy decisions to make. Not everyone can go with you where you are to go. Also, at the same time, you cannot go with others where they are destined to go in their God-called ministry. It goes both ways. Do not be a hindrance to another person's growth. Do not block the ministry they are called to fulfill.

Ministry does not need to be across the world. It can be to the neighbor next door or at an after-school yard program for children. Ministry may be to the senior or community food bank. Ministry may be making birthday parties for foster kids in group homes or battered women and men in shelters. Start where you are now. It may be in your hometown, or ministry may take you across the world.

Explore some of other Bible people who fulfilled their God destiny: prostitutes, murderers, and liars are included in the list: Daniel, Esther, Ruth, Joseph, Jesus, Peter, Andrew, Rahab, John the Baptist, Paul also known as Saul.

Keep your lamp plugged in to the world around you. Recognize when people need your input. Do not force your opinion on others. Live a life that is a witness. Be faithful to God and the calling God has given you. You have an assignment. God wants you to fulfill the assignment He has given you. Even when you have lived in chaos, your story can become a blessing to others. Always do the best to treat yourself well.

Each book includes a card that you send to yourself. Look for it at the end of this book. It's on the tear-off labeled "This card is for."

THE WRITER'S STORY

I do not want to tell you of disaster and chaos. It was surely there and would be a true story. It is more important to tell you of how God turned chaos in to victory.

This is a God story.

I was born the second child. I was a girl. The home already had a girl and wanted the second child to be a boy. My name as a boy was to be Conrad. This is the name I was called all my young life. Every day I was told that I was stupid and I was unwanted because I was not a boy.

I was also told that I was no good because I was just like my biological father who had left the home when I was four.

He was no good, and I was just like him. I was told that I was hated. There was also physical abuse for all the children in the home by my biological mother. In my opinion, a brother four years younger than I received the worst abuse. We were told how bad we were to be like our father who had left.

Child welfare stepped in and removed me from the home.

I heard my biological mother screaming to the judge, "I do not want her. I want her dead. She is dead." She left the judge's chambers as I was sent in the hall of the court.

The Arizona courts reached out to my biological father. He agreed to take me into his home. Three days prior to me moving in with him, he came to my school. I was called into the school office.

I was told by my father that he was now married and that I could not move in with him. His new wife of one year has three children, and he will raise them, but she does not want any children from his first marriage. I was told because I was my mother's child, I would not be able to come and live with them.

Okay. My mother does not want me because I am my father's child and not a boy.

My father says he can't take me because I am my mother's child.

What was my crime? I was born.

Fifty years later, I was still not allowed at my father's house. He is in his eighties now. He has told me that when he dies, I will not be listed as a child of his. I also will not be able to come to the funeral. He has promised me that I will be told of his passing, but how can he fulfill that promise after he has died? I cannot go to his home or see him or send him a card on Father's Day or see him at any holidays. His wife checks the phone to see if we talked. It became best that I do not reach out to him at all. It became too painful. He was a seed donor, and I am alive because of him.

He has told me that I was replaced with his three stepchildren, two girls and a boy. They attended private schools growing up. He owned his own business and paid for the school tuition. Money was never the factor of my not being able to live with him. I was told that his new wife wanted his stepchildren to meet the right people. It was important to attend private schools and meet all the right people.

He also was able to tell me about my birth. He said my biological mother did not want a girl. She would not even touch me until I was six months old. She hated me. He said she also abused him, my father, and he left because of that abuse.

He said he did not take me because men did not take their children in the 1950s and 1960s.

He also told me, when I was in my twenties, that the church I attended is where his neighbors also attended. His neighbors could not learn about me; they only knew of the children he and his new wife had. I was a secret. I did not exist.

This is the same beautiful church of Gospel Echoes where I learned how to pray. This is where I first started hearing that God saw me as valuable. It took another twenty years for me to believe that God did see me as valuable. I had to break the words that had been spoken over me. Words are damaging and can become a curse on any child's future.

As a child, I went very hungry. I had illness related to the malnutrition and abuse. My nose had been broken so many times as a child that the damage could only be corrected by removing all the bones in my nose in 1993. Today there are still signs of the missing bones.

I went through a marriage that was abusive and left after eighteen years. God wants a man to love his wife as Christ loves the church. Never demand in your rigidity of religion that a person who is abused should stay and take the abuse. That is not God. Moses was divorced. Never condemn someone for leaving an abuser. Help them as they leave, if you can. The abused return because they don't think they can make it financially and alone. They grow to believe they caused or deserve the abuse. I was a victim no more. I am a child of God.

God is a forgiving God of all sins. Divorce is not the unforgivable sin. You are able to remarry. Any divorce is covered by the blood when you ask for forgiveness. Why should a divorced person have to pay a higher price for leaving a sin that is already covered by the blood? Why should a person who is experiencing any form of abuse have to stay? They are free to remarry if God later brings them a Godly relationship. We cannot limit God and punish a divorced person. No matter why they are divorced, it is not listed as the unforgivable sin in the Bible.

I paid a big price to leave the abuse, spending nine months in shelters and eighteen months homeless. God is good. I never had to sleep on the street. I did go hungry and lost thirty pounds. I left with just the clothes on my back and went without a car for years.

I am not remarried. I am alone a lot but rarely lonely. I do see the rejection from believers toward many who are divorced and single and want to remarry. After I left, my ex-husband quickly remarried. (He professed to be a believer and worked for a TV ministry in another state.)

Being single is a choice at this time. I enjoy being a single person and have the freedom to minister to the hurting, being able to do workshops, give speeches, and my favorite thing, being able to pray for the healing of those in attendance, praying for those who have seen trauma. I also fought to raise the money to write and publish the *Burning Fires* workbook. It is my God assignment. The price was to live on a limited income and use food banks until this book was finished. I could not have taken someone else down this narrow road of sacrifices.

The *Burning Fires: Finding Treasures in Ashes* is an assignment that I had to complete. The workbook came from the hand of God. He did the healing and teaching in me first.

This is not a victim story. It is a God story. I see the hand of God, how He has taken a child who grew up in poverty who was deeply wounded and rejected by both parents, born a girl not a boy and told she was stupid all her life by parents and then an abusive spouse. She eventually learned of how much God saw her and does love her. He has orchestrated a ministry to bring healing to the many others who have experienced trauma.

No, this is not a victim story. If I had not lived through the chaos, I would not be able to speak into so many people's lives or tell them that God can heal all the hurt. Do I ever want to live it again? No. I am grateful that He is the healer. God is the provider, and He does love much and value every person. I can truly say to them that they are loved. God has anointed me to pray for the healing of their pain. I see them released into the fulness of God. I tell stories given to me by God. He is still a creative God, and we are made in His image to create also.

I get to tell stories of sixty-seven Chevrolets being restored and carrots that you have to wait to pull. I see the creation of God in the stars, and I am always at *awe* that He named me and calls me by name, just as He calls all of His stars by name.

He has taught me how to enter His throne room and spend time with Him. He has let me grow up in His throne room. I did not know I was growing up in His throne room until He showed me that He was my father. Growing up in His throne room will be the second book, which is already named "When God Is the Only Father."

In Revelation 2:17, it says we will be given a new name. Peter received a new name. Paul received a new name. Abraham received a new name. I received a new name. The courts changed my name legally to protect me from my abusive ex-husband. God really wanted to give me my new name. I got to pick the new name. God showed me what it was to be. It is the most beautiful name in the world. All three names were chosen because of their meaning. The old name is a sealed record. So, don't ask. The little abused girl no longer exists. I am a new creation in God—no longer hungry or rejected. I have a purpose to fulfill. You do too!

REFERENCES

NASB: New American Study Bible (1960, 1962, 1963, 1968, 1971, 1972, 1973, 1975, 1977). The Lockman Foundation: A corporation not for profit, La Habra, CA.

NIV: Life Application Study Bible (1991). New International Version. Tyndale House Publishers, Inc.: Wheaton Illinois. Zondervan.

All other Bible references were taken from computer website: Biblegateway.com.

Ronald Reagan. "Future does not belong to the fainthearted, it belongs to the Brave." President Ronald Reagan's speech, January 28, 1986. The *Challenger* space tragedy.

Amy Grant produced the song "My Fathers Eyes" released in 1979. In 2003, she produced the "I'm Gonna Fly" released in 2008. Zach Williams's song "Fear is a Liar" was released in 2016.

Pastor TD Jakes said during one of his broadcasts (paraphrased from TBN broadcast October 2019), "Your problem is the bridge to your success. You cannot avoid problems. Problems bridge us to the other side."

TD Jakes Ministries.

The Potter's House Church, Dallas Texas.

THIS CARD IS FOR:

"ME"

This Card is from Me,

I wanted to mail this card and say,

"What a great job in making that tough decision."

You are moving forward and,

You never give up!

Sometimes life has been hard,

But you are making it,

And are stronger today.

Yes, this card is for me—

And it is sent to me.

It has a stamp and was put in the mail.

I enjoyed it the day it was sent,

But enjoyed it more the day it arrived.

Not pretending it is from anyone else.

Just to remind only me, how special I am.

And to say,

"HAVE A NICE DAY!!"

CPSIA information can be obtained
at www.ICGtesting.com
Printed in the USA
LVHW050831200422
716608LV00007B/808